$\mathcal{R}$ISING FROM DEFEAT

The Overcomer's Handbook

By

Sherry Anderson

Jean –
Be all you can be!

Sherry

xulon PRESS

Cover design by Micah Gay / mdghipraz@gmail.com

www.xulonpress.com

Acknowledgements

Thank you to my husband, Mike, who has loved me through it all.
We've had quite a journey together!

Thank you to my faithful intercessors
Désirée, Orit, Suzanne, Esther, Bonnie, Carol, Debra, and Natalie
You helped me tremendously with this project.
I couldn't have done it without you.

Many thanks for inspiration and support go to Quin Sherrer,
my writing mentor.

Thank you Writer's Aglow friends for critique, love and prayers!

Introduction

*I*t is my hope that you are greatly encouraged as you read this book. It is interactive. By that I mean I share experiences and some scriptural exhortation and then there are places where you are given the opportunity to respond and apply these truths to your own life. If you want to, you can be greatly helped by what is written here. You will learn about the power of choice.

I have had more than my fair share of defeat! The good news is there can still be victory. The requirement is that we get back up after being knocked down. For me the frustration of defeat revealed itself in marriage, parenthood, prayer-life, relationships, business, ministry, and the inability to even use my talents and abilities. Many times I would attempt to rise only to experience setback once again.

With our human reasoning, we deduce that God expects some kind of victorious performance as we encounter challenges and trials in our lives. I found that I did not know God very well. He is not like I imagined Him to be. He is more loving, more powerful, more patient, more to be reverenced, more to be respected, and more awesome than I ever envisioned Him to be. It has been in getting to know Him that I have found the freedom to be myself, to be honest with Him, and to depend on His strength for everything. In my weakness, He has become strong!

I am learning about the grace of God. I have known for a long time what I should do, but could not do it. At times I've thought the Lord was disappointed in me because I had not done what I knew was His revealed will. But He knew I could not do it. He patiently waited while I made the discovery. The bottom line: I have found the secret of overcoming to be personal humility and the grace of God. "God resists the proud and gives grace to the humble."

It is my sincere prayer that my experiences as set forth in this book, along with the scriptural answers, will give hope to all who read them and that hope will give way to faith so you, too, can arise in His power!

TABLE OF CONTENTS

Chapter 14

Chapter 15

Chapter 16

Section Three: HOW TO MOVE ON

Chapter 17

Chapter 18

Chapter 19

Chapter 20

Chapter 21

Chapter 22

Chapter 23

Chapter 24

SECTION ONE:
DEALING WITH OURSELVES

Chapter 1

The Power of Choice

One of the most important things we need to learn is the power of making a choice. Every choice adds up to success or failure. It is the sum of these decisions that determines our direction and whether our destiny will be fulfilled.

Get Over It

It usually isn't our own idea that we need to "get over it." Typically, someone else points it out. Perhaps we were reliving a bad experience by telling it once again. Or they may see that we aren't doing something we really want to do because of what happened last time. It is then that we hear those words, "Get over it!" I feel that if someone is going to tell us to get over it, they should at least tell us *how*.

How do we get beyond the way we were treated by people and damaged by things that happened in our lives? That is what this book is all about: learning how to overcome. To overcome is to conquer, beat, master something, win, and be victorious!

So I am saying to you in a kind way, using a nice tone of voice, you really need to get over it. You need to get over your disappointments, how people treated you, even your bad choices. In this book I am going to show how you can get over it according to God's Word. You then have a choice as to whether you will go through the process and move on in your life. But, if time goes by, and you are still reliving your old grievances and refuse to follow the instructions, I have the right to say in a stern tone "*Get over it!*" My tone of voice will change because you will know *how* and it will be your own fault if you are miserable or stuck somewhere!

I invite you to discover how I conquered rejection, fear, unbelief, and many other things and to apply the same principles to your life. Come on, you *can* get over it!

I asked the Lord to show me how I began to rise from defeat and get over the things that had happened to me. This was what He said to me.

- You started to get over it when you *listened* to Me.
- You started to get over it when you *applied* the Truth to your life.
- You started to get over it when you had eyes to see and ears to hear. (Religion makes us deaf and blind to what is truly going on spiritually.)
- You started to get over it when you no longer chased meetings, teachers, and gifts, and began to seek Me and My company and My presence.

- You started to get over it when you began to really *hope* in Me.

- You started to get over it when you took people off the pedestal and put Me there!

How To Get Over Yourself

I've heard people say to others, "Oh, get *over* yourself." They usually meant that a person was putting too much importance on themselves or getting easily offended. But this chapter is written to address what it is about ourselves that holds us back from being all we can be: the fearful, condemning, unforgiving, criticizing voices from within.

In order to make progress, we must deal with:

If only I hadn't...

If only I had...

Regrets, grief, remorse?

I wish I hadn't...

I wish I had...

Did you mess up?

Have you wasted years of your life?

Did you do foolish things as a teenager?

Did you have an abortion, or pay for someone to obtain one?

You can get over it!

If You Change Your Mind, It Will Change Your Life!

My Story

After reading back over what I had written in my journals in the past ten years, it was obvious that I was always repenting for the same things and continued to deal with fear, unbelief, low self-esteem, and procrastination. So many times, the Lord spoke to me concerning what was hindering me, and I would write it in my journal and turn the page and go on. What began to change my life was when I took what the Lord said to me through the Scriptures or what He spoke to me in my spirit and began to declare it daily until it changed my mind by replacing wrong thoughts with the truth of God's Word.

This is the impact: when I change my mind, the words that come out of my mouth will be different. When I change what I am declaring with my mouth, my life will be different! I found this out for myself. The Scriptural basis for this is found in Romans 12:2a (NASB) where we are admonished, *And do not be conformed to this world, but be transformed by the renewing of your mind.* A transformation of my life began to take place as I applied this principle to my life.

Why did declaring what the Lord said have such an impact? There is much power in the tongue! Here is what the Bible says about it:

We all stumble in many ways. If anyone is never at fault in what he says, he is a perfect man, able to keep his whole body in check. When we put bits into the mouths of horses to make them obey us, we can turn the whole animal. Or take ships as an example. Although they are so large and are driven by strong winds, they are steered by a very small rudder wherever the pilot wants to go. (James 3:2-4 NIV 1984)

I discovered my tongue could steer me just like the rudder of a ship! It could steer my life in God's direction and His plans for me or in the direction the enemy plans for my life. It was time to choose!

Likewise the tongue is a small part of the body, but it makes great boasts. Consider what a great forest is set on fire by a small spark. The tongue also is a fire, a world of evil among the parts of the body. It corrupts the whole person, sets the whole course of his life on fire, and is itself set on fire by hell. All kinds of animals, birds, reptiles and creatures of the sea are being tamed and have been tamed by man, but no man can tame the tongue. It is a restless evil, full of deadly poison. With the tongue we praise our Lord and Father, and with it we curse men, who have been made in God's likeness. Out of the same mouth come praise and cursing. My brothers, this should not be. Can both fresh water and saltwater flow from the same spring? (James 3:5-11 NIV 1984)

We have power to speak life or death. Death is produced by agreeing with the negative thoughts and vocalizing them. This gives the enemy permission to torment us, and in reality we are speaking word-curses over ourselves, others, our church, job, or business.

Jesus had something to say about what comes out of our mouth:

For out of the abundance of the heart the mouth speaks. A good man out of the good treasure of his heart brings forth good things, and an evil man out of the evil treasure brings forth evil things. But I say to you that for every idle word men may speak, they will give account of it in the day of judgment. For by your words you will be justified, and by your words you will be condemned. (Matthew 12:34b-37 NKJ)

He also said in Matthew 15:11 (NKJ): *Not what goes into the mouth defiles a man; but what comes out of the mouth, this defiles a man.*

By our words we agree with God or else we reinforce the bad things that we think and feel. How do you talk to yourself when no one is listening? Are you speaking kindly, encouraging yourself, or are you cutting yourself down and speaking negatively? Are you muttering under your breath about the way someone has treated you? Are you telling and retelling to others what has happened to you? There is power released with the words!

So, where do you begin to make the change? Words have already been spoken from your lips that have released curses. The word-curses must be broken and the enemy must be driven out. The real warfare begins with being honest with ourselves and with God. Have you been angry and out of control? As long as we are blaming someone else for what we are doing, we cannot be set free from it. Repentance brings deliverance.

You may have had problems for so long that it is hard to believe you could be set free. Let me share a story with you. A circus trainer bought a baby elephant. Knowing the elephant would one day grow to be a large and powerful creature, he wanted to train him that he could only go so far. He tied the small animal's ankle by a rope to a stake, so that he was unable to walk away. Whenever the elephant tried to break free, it would only hurt him, so he learned to stay tethered.

As the elephant grew, the trainer kept a rope tied around his ankle that wasn't tied to anything, but the elephant did not walk away because he didn't know he could. The rope on his ankle always reminded him of his previous limitations. He grew up to be tremendous in size and very powerful, but didn't know he was free to walk away.

This happens in our lives, too. We get out of the circumstances and situations that we had in the past. The people are out of the picture or at least the circumstances have changed, but the rope around our ankle that we had at a younger age fools us into thinking we cannot walk away from the captivity, or emotions that we had in the past.

Break the Spell!

It takes using our faith. The Bible says that we all have been given a measure of faith so we must use our faith to believe that God will heal us if we will face these things. Some of us will say, "I don't want to deal with things – I don't want to *go* there!" But there is a freedom that comes in dealing with all this stuff.

It is wonderful to get to the place where we only respond to what happened to us today, not the mountain of hurt and disappointment that happened in our lifetime. That can only happen if we get rid of the mountain. So it takes the faith that God has given us and that faith may not look like much, but that mustard seed of faith is enough. A mustard seed is very, very small – about the size of the head of a pin. Jesus said that it would move mountains if we use it.

Then we must use our free-will – the enemy cannot take it away from us. We make a choice to do the will of God.

This book is interactive. Right now you can follow the instructions and "get over yourself." Set your will in that direction. Use that little tiny bit of faith and you can be restored, but it is messy having to do it. You may cry as you deal with things, but all you have to do while you are dealing with these things is be honest with God. Tell Him how you feel. (He really knows already). We must choose to forgive ourselves and let things go.

Make this declaration: I *will* be made whole!

Prayer: I forgive myself for everything I have ever done and for everything I *haven't* done that I should have done.

Note:

Many times things come up that you have vowed never to forgive yourself for. If you feel that rise up within you, say, "Lord, help me to forgive myself." Then repeat the opening line to this prayer again and you will be able to forgive yourself. God is so good to help us in every situation.

Maybe this list will help brings things to your memory that you need to forgive yourself for. Pause after each question to see if something comes to mind. Then say, I forgive myself for _____ (fill in the blank).

- What did you do that you regret so much?
- What did you say that you wish you hadn't said?
- Did you have an abortion or pay for someone to have one?
- Was there a decision you made that sent you on the wrong course?
- Did you stay when you should have gone or leave when you should have stayed?
- What bad choice did you make?
- Take your time and name the things you are forgiving yourself for.
- Then ask the Lord to heal your disappointment in yourself.
- Maybe you have a broken heart over what you did. Ask the Lord to heal it.

Declaration: I break every word-curse off my life that has been spoken by me, by family, friends, and enemies, in Jesus name.

Note:

I break the word-curses off my life every day.

We break our alliance with the enemy through repentance, and this is where to start. We must make Jesus Lord over our own life in order to walk this out, otherwise, we slip right back to where we were. The Word also says, *Therefore, submit to God. Resist the devil, and he will flee from you.* (James 4:7 NKJ) Submitting to God is of the utmost importance in order to get free. The Lord does His part if we will do ours!

Prayer: Lord, I submit my life to You and will be honest with myself and You. Lord, I pray for all self-justification, reasoning, excuses, procrastination, and self-deception about the condition of my own heart to be removed in Jesus name. I renounce all cooperation with the enemy by defending myself and saying I'm really not that bad when I compare myself to others. God, I want to respond to You without making excuses.

Lord, I have been angry, unforgiving, and I've wanted to get even. I'm hurt and disappointed. I repent for these things and am depending on You to heal and deliver me.

Lord, I forgive _____. (Be specific about the people you need to forgive.

Or your problem could be, Lord, I have been afraid to trust You and have not been obedient to what I know You have told me to do. (Everyone is dealing with something, so just be honest about it.)

Chapter 2

How I Got Over the Things That Happened to Me

But to you who fear My name, the Sun of Righteousness shall arise with healing in His wings. And you shall go out and grow fat like stall-fed calves. (Malachi 4:2 NKJ)

A Woman's Story

One evening at a women's ministry meeting, our guest speaker shared her story of being sexually molested as a child. She had been through some terrible abuse and as a result of it, she grew up with a variety of emotional and relationship problems. Then she said "I made a choice to get over it!" Through inner healing and deliverance, it no longer haunted her. She shared how she made the decision to overcome it and not let it hinder the rest of her life and her relationship with her husband. She allowed the Lord to heal her memories and emotions, and she got rid of her baggage.

My Story

I had not been through anything as bad as she had so I decided if she could get over all that, I could get over my stuff, too! I went home that night and asked the Lord what was hindering me spiritually and why I could not seriously commit to the church I was attending. As I was praying about this, I got honest with God and wrote in my journal:

"Although there were some good things in my previous church experiences, I've also been hurt, disappointed, rejected, humiliated, scorned, talked about, hated, misunderstood, ignored, tolerated and abused in ministry. This has kept me from wanting any more ministry involvement, but I am ready to get over it! Heal me and I will be truly healed."

I wrote: "Regarding my life – Lord, I receive Your healing for all my disappointments. I receive healing for all my failure and give up grieving over my mistakes. I forgive myself. I let it all go!" I declared, "I'm cherished and loved. I'm forgiven, accepted and this is a new day for me in God." I knew if my disappointments and failure were brought up again, it was not the Lord doing it!

I told the Lord: "Regarding Bible study and quiet time/prayer: I've set goals many times and failed miserably. I've fallen asleep, been lazy, passive, apathetic, and bored, and I'm ready to get over it!" I lifted my hands and said, "I receive the power, the grace, the help, the discipline that I need."

In relationships: "I've been taken for granted, used, misunderstood, ignored, lied to, abused, intimidated, and I'm ready to get over it!"

In business: "I've been deceived, given away money foolishly, been bankrupt, in arrears, looked down on, intimidated, fearful, and made to feel inferior. I have failed miserably, but I'm ready to get over it! Heal my mind (I placed my hands on my head) and my heart (laid my hand on my heart)." I lifted my hands and said, "I receive wisdom, faith, favor, grace, abundant blessing, and guidance."

In ministry: "I've been ignored. I've been disappointed in myself. I've been passive, lazy, and lacked faith. I've been abused, abandoned, and used. But I'm getting over it! I'm through with the old pattern, old stumbling blocks and old excuses. I'm going on with my life!"

Regarding healing: "I've made a fool of myself. I've had people die that I thought would be healed and people nearly always stayed sick when I prayed for them. I've been confused and unbelieving. But I'm getting over it!"

In witnessing: "I've been ridiculed, rejected, then became lazy, apathetic, complacent, and a failure. I'm getting over it!"

In hearing the voice of God: "I've been deceived, confused, lazy, apathetic, unbelieving, and disobedient. I'm getting over it! Heal me and deliver me! Lord, You can do it. I'm *letting* You do it."

The Lord is so faithful. He healed me of all I asked Him to! By being honest with Him and making a choice to get over the things that happened, the process of restoration began in all these areas of my life.

I will exalt You, O LORD,

for You lifted me out of the depths

and did not let my enemies gloat over me.

O LORD my God, I called to You for help

and You healed me.

O LORD, You brought me up from the grave;

You spared me from going down into the pit.

Sing to the LORD, you saints of His;

praise His holy name. (Psalm 30:1-4 NIV)

Issues from the Past Causing Problems in the Present

My Story

He was tall, dark, and handsome! I was twelve, he was fourteen, and all my friends knew I liked him a lot. As he approached the school bus every day, they would chant, "Here comes Sher – ry's boy – friend, here comes Sher – ry's boy – friend!"

One day I got the nerve up to write him a note. It probably went something like this, "I like you. Do you like me? Here is my school picture." I gave it to him in the morning on the way to school and couldn't wait to see what he would write in a note back to me. As he was getting off the bus by his house that afternoon, he dropped a folded paper in my lap as he walked by. My heart raced as I waited for the bus to arrive at my stop where I could read the note privately.

As the bus pulled away, I opened the folded paper and out fell my picture. The note read, "If you will grow up and stop embarrassing me, then I *might* consider you." I was devastated. As I came through the front door crying, my mother said, "Well, what's wrong with you?" "This," I said as I tossed my note in front of her on the table and ran to my bedroom. She never said a word to me about it and I cried myself to sleep that night. No one comforted me.

Placing myself in a vulnerable position by revealing my true feelings resulted in having them crushed. I made up my mind that it would not happen again. A wall went up that would hinder me from really falling in love as an adult. Looking back, the events of a twelve year-old girl do not seem like they would be so earth-shattering. But to the child that I was so many years ago, it was real. It was painful, and its baggage came with me into the present. I promised myself that this would never happen again. This is what I refer to as an "inner vow." I was not even conscious of what I was doing. I made this vow to protect myself from a degree of hurt or rejection, but it also began the construction of a wall that would keep me from being able to receive or give love.

Looking back over my life, I discovered that during my adolescent years I made a number of decisions that brought a degree of protection from harm, but also a great deal of restriction. At moments of emotional pain, we tend to vow inwardly never to put ourselves in that position again, or to trust again, or whatever fits the situation. Many times it is years later before we realize that the problems that we have in current relationships can be traced back to painful times in our past. It seems that as humans, we are doing the best we can to survive. We believe that all these methods we use are quite normal when we compare ourselves with each other. It is only as the Lord reveals what is truly going on that we face the issues. A good thing to remember is "What the Lord reveals, He heals." He doesn't bring up our past to remind us of our sins or to have us repent over and over. He only brings up things to set us free from their negative effects on us.

I remember the first time I heard a guest speaker mention walls that we put up to protect ourselves. This was a revelation to me and I prayed for the walls to come down while I was at the Aglow retreat. I came home and shared this with my husband and he said, "Oh, we *all* have walls." I thought to myself, "*You* have walls?" I had never noticed his because I couldn't see over mine! These walls are invisible but are very real. We erect them because we have been hurt or disappointed and want to protect ourselves from it ever happening again.

One way to erect a wall is by making a vow to yourself, "I'll never share my true feelings with someone again." Or "No one will ever do that to me again!" As a result of these vows, we keep a degree of hurt out, but also prevent intimacy with others. My definition of intimacy is being able to share heart to heart. I share my heart and thoughts with someone and they open up the same to me. The greatest harm that can be done to intimacy is when that trust is broken.

Most of us can think back to our childhood and remember a time that we confided in a friend and told them a secret. Later someone else came back to us and knew the secret. Our friend had broken our trust. Maybe we tried again with someone else and again were hurt this way. Before we knew it, it was impossible to share our true feelings with a friend and we said to ourselves, "If this is what friends do, who needs them?"

When I was around fourteen years old, I had a boyfriend who decided he liked my best friend more than me and the two of them started seeing each other behind my back. It was then that I decided that I really didn't need a close friend. Another friend stole my favorite necklace. I never trusted friends after that.

My father was in the military and we moved every few years. I assumed that because my friends changed periodically due to moves, that surface relationships were quite normal. As an adult I've had casual friendships with many people, never allowing myself to become vulnerable enough to be hurt by them. When disappointed, I would say to myself, "I'm too mature to let something like this upset me." I truly believed that this was the mature way of dealing with conflict. It turned out as an adult that I had a lot of issues that were not dealt with and I had pushed down my anger to the point that I was totally unaware that I was angry at anyone about anything! This was exposed to the light a few years ago.

When I was nineteen years old someone I loved died suddenly. This affected me deeply in a negative way. In my mind, it seemed that either someone would break your heart or die. I began to think to myself, "Why get your heart involved in relationships? You will only get hurt in the end." After being hurt a number of times, I decided that the pain wasn't worth the risk I would have to take to have close relationships. After becoming a Christian, the Lord told me one day that I was stoic. So I looked up the word in a dictionary to see what it meant. In essence it means unable to show emotion.

But it was even deeper than that. I would not *let* myself feel emotion, much less show it!

I felt the mature thing was not to let petty things that people did affect me. I felt it was juvenile to let things "get to me." What I didn't realize was that in doing this, I had a lot of unresolved issues. While I thought I was not letting things bother me, they were still deeply affecting me and causing a moodiness that would come over me unexpectedly. Later I discovered that anger would also lift its ugly head. I had previously made forgiveness a lifestyle for myself. I chose to forgive others regardless of the offense. This was because of the Lord's Prayer which says "Forgive us our trespasses as we forgive those who trespass against us." This means forgive me the same way I forgive others. I certainly wanted the Lord to wipe my slate clean!

I didn't realize that I had only half of the information I needed to overcome the negative things that people did to me. Forgiving people was only part of what I needed to do. I also needed the hurt to be healed. I didn't know that I was in denial. I really thought it was being handled in a mature way and that I could just choose not to let these things bother me. However, hurtful words do hurt. Rejection hurts. Being overlooked hurts. Having someone be unfaithful to you hurts. When someone doesn't believe your words, it hurts. When people talk about you, it hurts. Whether you are in touch with the pain or not, the hurt is there and it is real. Sooner or later the lid to the barrel of unresolved issues is going to come off! And when it does, we have a choice of whether to stuff it back in there and force the lid on till another day or decide it is time to "deal."

Dealing with the barrel of unresolved issues is a process not a "poof" by the wand of the *Amazing Jesus*. Sometimes we wish He was a magician, but emptying the barrel involves honesty, repentance, forgiveness, prayer, healing, and deliverance.

Take the time to pray for the Holy Spirit to bring up an unresolved issue. Something may have already come to your mind while reading this. Here are steps that will help to resolve what needs to be dealt with.

Step 1: Face it and be honest with yourself about how the incident made you feel. This could be painful to face and deal with. But ask the Lord to help you. This is not a "re-hash" session. By that I mean it won't need to be brought up over and over again in the course of your life. If this is dealt with it will never need to be brought up again!

Step 2: Admit it if the incident humiliated, hurt, or injured you. Ask the Lord to show you if incidents in your past caused you to make vows to yourself. Give yourself time to see if memories come up while you are praying.

Step 3: In order to break a vow that was made, you can pray a prayer like this:

"Lord, I repent for making a vow to (example: never trust again...or always keep my distance...). I break the power of the words I spoke over myself and I ask You to deliver me from the bondage that came into my life at that time. Heal me of (name what happened then) and I forgive (name the one(s) who hurt you). Thank You for setting me free!

Chapter 3

Doubt, Unbelief & Fear

Though one may be overpowered by another, two can withstand him. And a threefold cord is not quickly broken. (Ecclesiastes 4:12 NKJ)

This Scripture states the principle that there is strength in numbers. The principle is true whether for good or evil. These three things – doubt, unbelief, and fear – work together to bring defeat to a Christian's life.

How did I, as a Christian, go from walking in faith to being totally shut down? Being ignorant of the tactics of the enemy is how it happened to me.

Be sober, be vigilant; because your adversary the devil walks about like a roaring lion, seeking whom he may devour. (1 Peter 5:8 NKJ)

The Enemy Called Doubt

As God's people, we are to *be transformed by the renewing of your mind* (Romans 12:2 NKJ).

I am convinced that we have to change our thinking with the Word of God to be immune to attacks in our thought life. Because we have been ignorant of this fact and are not prepared, we don't respond correctly when the thoughts come. Nothing has changed with the enemy. Satan still uses the question he used in the Garden of Eden, "Has God *really* said?"

Your word I have hidden in my heart that I might not sin against You. (Psalm 119:11 NKJ)

I did not realize that doubt was a sin. It only seemed that doubting was a weakness, so I did not address it for what it was – something to repent of. If I had renewed my mind to agree with what God said, either through the Scriptures or a *rhema* word, I would have won the battle at this level. Because in some areas, I hadn't renewed my mind, I had a struggle to keep believing. It took a while, but a subtle change came and I lost my footing. Paul, in his letter to the Ephesians, tells us to put on the *whole* armor of God. The helmet is to protect the mind. Oops! Where is my helmet? The middle of a battle is no time to be searching for pieces of my armor! I grabbed my shield of faith and thought I was fighting the best possible way. I was ignorant because it also takes the sword of the Spirit, the Word of God, to win this fight. Instead, I hung on to hope and tried to believe. At this point, I was a soldier in a defensive position and eventually was worn down trying to fight off negative thoughts. My enemy was persistent. So...

I Encountered My Next Enemy Called Unbelief

I graduated from doubt to unbelief. In this battle, to graduate is to descend from where I was to a lower plane in the spirit. Unbelief is a slimy pit. All I had to do was doubt and I slid right into it.

In my early Spirit-filled days, I did some pretty bold things. I had crazy faith and became disappointed when those presumptuous things didn't turn out like I thought they would. The Lord has no obligation to honor prayers and do things that do not originate with Him and His will. Presumption is "presuming to know." I look back now and I did not know very much – I only thought I did!

As a result of this crazy faith, the enemy eventually caused me to doubt the Word of God and the faithfulness of God. I was not aware of this taking place. Back then, there was something called the "faith movement." It ended up getting out of balance, and people were "naming and claiming" fancy cars and all sorts of greedy things. I got so disgusted with it that I threw the whole faith message out. God's Word is true, of course, but carnal Christians saw it as an opportunity for personal gain, and so the message became perverted by wrong motives.

The Bible says, *Delight yourself also in the Lord, And He shall give you the desires of your heart.* (Psalm 37:4 NKJ) That kind of relationship takes time. As I delight myself in Him, the desires are changed and I begin to want the things that He wants, and then what I desire is good for me in the long run.

I have coined a phrase that I call "*one-day* faith." For example: "*One* day I will write a book" or "*One* day I will pray more." The Bible says "Today is the day of salvation!" *One-day* faith is just another form of procrastination and is not faith at all! It is a comfortable, non-risky stance and is unbelief masquerading as faith. Days went by. Months went by. And before I knew it, years went by. I thought that I was waiting on God to come through for me. This kind of waiting is passivity and is also an enemy, and prevents us from doing anything about the condition we are in. Passivity is a counterfeit "rest." I still believed what God said was true and that *someday* both the written Word and the prophetic words we had received would materialize. I just knew that *one day* God would do what He had promised. God's promises and prophetic words to us are conditional. That means we cannot afford to be passive. He is looking for cooperation from us and He is expecting us to mature in the process.

It Was Not Long Until I Slipped Into Fear

Fear is a "partner in crime" with doubt and unbelief. Because, after sliding into the pit, fear with subtlety says, "If you try to believe God again, aren't you afraid that nothing will happen when you pray just like before?" or "What if the same things happen if you commit to this church that happened at the last one? What if you are rejected by people again?" Fear was my slime-pit companion! Fear can also be recognized by thoughts like: "What if this whole thing is a mistake?" "Have I wasted my whole life believing in something that will never happen?" "What if God doesn't come through?" "What if it is too late?" "What if…?" "What if nothing changes?" "What if I don't get healed?" Fear paralyzes.

Fear causes us to withdraw to safety. I found myself in a cave and didn't care if I *ever* came out. I refer to a place of passivity, complacency, and waiting as "the cave." It is comfortable in the cave. Another descriptive title is "comfort zone." Once in there I felt safe. I liked being in the background again. It doesn't take any faith to stay there. It is the path of least resistance. I became a spectator in the house of God instead of a participant.

Facing the Giant of Fear

My Story

When I was growing up, I had a big fear problem. I was afraid of the dark and imagined all sort of things were lurking there. My grandmother's house was built before there were indoor bathroom facilities. So at some point, they added onto the house off from the kitchen a room with an adjoining bathroom. In order to get to the bathroom at night, we had to go through the dark room. My sister and I were both afraid of the dark but sometimes would hide from each other and jump out as the other one emerged from the bathroom into the pitch-black darkness. We did it just to scare each other and watch each other collapse as our knees gave out.

It seems fear is addictive, because I would pick up a *TV Guide* magazine and flip through it and in a matter of moments knew all the scary things that would be on TV that week. It was thrilling to annually go through the Jaycee's Haunted House. When a scary movie came on TV, though terrified, I could not turn it off. Through things like this, I ended up with even more fear as an adult.

After being saved and baptized in the Holy Spirit, I began to wake up from a sound sleep, paralyzed by fear and could not move or speak. I was desperate and when I heard about a deliverance ministry decided to go for prayer because of the torment. One of the people praying for me said. "I see you about five years old, and

44

you are in your room at night, and there is a storm. A tree limb was beating against your window and you were either afraid to call out or if you called out, no one heard you." She described my haircut as kind of a "bowl" cut and that the curtains were embroidered. She prayed for me concerning this episode in my life and that the door would be closed to the enemy regarding fear.

That afternoon I called my mother and asked where we lived when I was five and what my haircut was like. I asked what kind of curtains were in my room. She replied, "I made your curtains and embroidered them." She had no idea why I was asking, but confirmed what the Holy Spirit had revealed. With this time of ministry, along with using Scriptures such as "The Lord has not given me a spirit of fear, but of power, love, and a sound mind," over a period of time I renewed my mind and am totally free from irrational fear. I avoid scary movies because I don't want to ever be tormented by fear again! I've told you this story to let you know that what God reveals, He heals. He revealed the root-cause of my fear, healed me and set me free.

Fear of Persecution

The disciples were accustomed to Jesus teaching, healing people, and performing signs and wonders. However, they had also seen the religious people accuse Him of blasphemy and of being possessed by a demon. After his crucifixion, resurrection, and ascension into heaven, a change came for the disciples and they became the ones doing the ministry. They were baptized in the Holy Spirit, then heard from God and obeyed. They had fruit *and* persecution. They became the ones being talked about.

Up until recent years I was content to be taught and ministered *to*. I was safe because I didn't *do* anything that would cause me to be talked about and rejected. I only did what was *safe*.

I sometimes dreaded people. I got to the place where the Lord even asked me to do something or say something to a person and I couldn't do it. Me, a mature Christian, not obey God? I thought *what is wrong with me*? My dread was: "What will they do? What will they think?"

Fear of Man

As long as we only do what is safe we won't be talked about and rejected like Jesus and His disciples were. The Fear of Man is a giant in our land. When we challenge it, we can expect it to make terrible noises to frighten us. It may try to growl us into submission, to cause us to back off because we're afraid to upset the applecart. This fear has kept me from expressing my true feelings because of fear that anger will rise up in another person and they would take my head off. Our battle is not against flesh and blood. Many times it is a spiritual conflict in our dealing with others that we are in relationship with. Our demons are warring against one another. I am not that person's real enemy, nor are they mine.

My Story

Fear of man (people) goes back to my childhood. I was sensitive to what was going on around me. When someone was angry, I didn't just hear their words, I *felt* their anger. My mother was the one I feared the most. She was a good mother and did the best she could, but was not someone you wanted mad at you. I saw her pick up whatever was at hand (for instance a broom or cooking spatula) and go after my brothers. Anger scared me. So fear made me a "follower," and I never wanted to provoke someone to lose their temper. I did not misbehave when I was a child because of the fear of Mama's angry reaction. I got married at age 17 to get away from home. Of five siblings, I was the only one who experienced this.

I lived with the spirit of fear – yielding and submitting to it. I started to fear others, and didn't want to do or say anything to cause them to become angry. When I did something wrong and their tempers arose, it wasn't just their words, but I could feel the anger pressing against me. It was as if it said to me, "You *better* back down. You don't want to see how ugly this can get!" So I always cowered.

Finally, in recent years I got angry at this giant of fear. I was angry that I let it rule me. I realized I did not have to live this way. Not only that, I decided I *will not* live this way. I dealt with it head-on with my words. "Spirits that cause me to fear anger, rejection, abandonment, retaliation, of being hurt further – I address you to your face. You will not rule my life! You are losing your hold over me now! Jesus is my Lord. I submit to Him and resist you and you must flee. I break your hold off my life. I renounce you. God hasn't given me a spirit of fear! I have power, love and a sound mind! I will not fear. Greater is He who is in me than he that is in the world! The righteous are as bold as a lion! With God all things are possible – facing this giant is *possible*! Nothing is too difficult for the Lord. This mess is not too difficult for the Lord to sort out and heal.

I said, "Oh God, I want off this train – so I'm getting off!" I decided to do what Jude wrote in Jude 1:3.

I found it necessary to write to you exhorting you to **contend earnestly** *for the faith which was once for all delivered to the saints.* (NKJ)

Then in Verse 20, he tells us how to contend.

But you, beloved, building yourselves up on your most holy faith, **praying in the Holy Spirit** (Jude 1:20 KJV).

Earnestly means get intensely serious. Contend means to struggle to deal with. I decided to fight for it! I made a choice to refuse letting the fear of people and what they will do, rule my life. Your fears may be different, but you can do the same thing and overcome them.

Choose to be set free!

The Cave

My Story

I never heard anyone mention "cave dwelling" until I was attending a conference one summer. The speaker said, "Some people have been in a cave so long they have decorated it, sprayed air freshener, and are pretending they are just fine." Uh-oh, God was talking to me! As I sat there, I realized I had retreated into the cave because of being hurt by those in spiritual authority above me. "How could I ever trust a leader over me again?" was the question I kept asking myself. Then the guest speaker said, "The only way to come out of the cave is to exit through the same door you entered. It could be fear, hurt, or failure that took you in." That meant facing what took me there, and being courageous was the way out. I knew this would be a significant decision and after four years of safety, I decided to come out!

Back at my home later that day, I looked around my living room. Every plant in the house had outgrown its container and become root bound. In nature, a plant's root system naturally extends three times the length that it does above ground. If a plant is not re-potted in a larger container, it will literally suffocate itself. I realized that the cave had become too cramped for me. Although it felt safe I wasn't growing anymore and I wanted so much more to take place in my life.

I wrote this in my journal at that time:

"I'm tired enough of this cramped place that I am willing to come out of the cave, my comfortable cave, to be no longer in control of my safety. I have scars but to be honest scars don't bleed and they're not sore. There is no pain in the scars themselves. So why look at the scars and fear more scars? Every scar can become a testimony."

As Christians, the more we grow and expand in ministry, the more we need to spend time daily with the Lord. It takes more to maintain what we have and to increase beyond what we have. In order to be strong in the Lord, we must be empowered by our union with Him.

In conclusion, be strong in the Lord [be empowered through your union with Him]; draw your strength from Him [that strength which His boundless might provides]. (Ephesians 6:10 AMP)

Now back to the cave...

My retreat into the cave was the result of experiencing hurt and betrayal from leaders in the church. This was compounded by other things that seemed to have gone wrong in my life. So for me coming out of the cave was to again submit to a leader and be vulnerable to hurt again. I had to pray through this, forgive again, and ask the Lord to heal everything and to help me make the steps that were needed.

I declared my freedom. I cried and went through more healing in order to do this. But I did it!

However as time goes by, there is a temptation to go back to the safety of a cave. But then I remember the famine, the desolation, and the frustration that was there. The Lord reminds me that I really don't want that for my life.

If you feel you are in a cave, ask yourself these questions: What took me in? And what will it take to come out? Your cave could have included an exit from the organized church or withdrawing from leadership, or even backsliding in your relationship with the Lord.

Pray: I forgive _____ and I forgive myself. I receive the courage and the grace to overcome this.

This was a difficult lesson for me. It turned out that I was once again disappointed and felt betrayed by a leader. God does not honor the "three strikes and you are out" baseball element we have added to His command to align with leaders. Yes, it was painful once again and back in the cave I went. The Lord led us to change to a different church and we got planted there. Once again after an extended period of time, I got miserable enough to come back out and become an active participant instead of a spectator in the house of God.

Cave dwelling may seem to be a life of freedom, but a cave is a cave. In the Old Testament, the Midianites caused Israel to dwell in caves, dens, and strongholds to protect themselves. That is usually the reason we retreat to a cave also. However, we were not created to be cave dwellers. We are to dwell under an open heaven, with crops being blessed and bringing increase. We are to have houses being blessed, not caves being blessed. Blessed coming in and going out (see Deuteronomy 28).

Deal with the Spirit of Unbelief

After a long period of time, I finally got miserable and desperate enough to do something. My cure for the condition I found myself in was to treat unbelief as an enemy. I could not get rid of fear as long as unbelief was plaguing me. I became aggressive against unbelief by repenting of it and renouncing it. It took fasting and declaring the truth in order to break its hold over me. I prayed in the Spirit one hour a day for a period of time.

But ye, beloved, building up yourselves on your most holy faith, praying in the Holy Spirit (Jude 1:20 ASV).

I wrote out a declaration to make it plain to myself and the spirit realm that I meant business! Declaring out loud what the Word said and what the Lord has spoken to me personally, built my faith and renewed my mind by replacing the wrong thoughts with the *Truth*! Defeating unbelief took care of fear and doubt also.

The Lord stirred my heart to **believe**! I discovered that He is looking for those who will just believe Him! I know this must sound so profoundly simple. But I heard someone once say, "The hardest thing to learn is the thing you thought you learned already." Now we need this simple message of faith and believing God or we cannot inherit the promises and enter the "promised land."

If I am going to walk with God, I must agree with God. *Can two walk together, unless they are agreed?* (Amos 3:3 NKJ) I cannot agree with God unless I know His thoughts on a matter. How can I know His thoughts on a matter? I can know by searching it out in the Scriptures with prayer and having a revelation of it. Then I choose by an act of my will to confess with my mouth what He has to say on a particular subject, i.e., healing, who I am in Him, and what He says about the future. That is the "faith" walk. Not dreaming up something I'm lusting after (worldly goods or an easy way out of my trials), but believing God's Word above what I see with my own eyes. Now that makes God happy! He gives us joy in believing. No wonder I felt heaviness instead of joy. I was waiting for something to happen in my life and it just wasn't happening. Was I waiting on God? Was I waiting for some special servant of God to pray for me to have a breakthrough? Was I waiting on a prophetic word to come forth over my life that would break the awful spell I had been under? It is sad to say, but I was waiting on something like that to happen and I had disappointment after disappointment. My deliverance didn't come from without, but instead it came from within! These spirits no longer have a hold on me. You can break the power of unbelief in your life too.

- Treat it as an enemy and stand aggressively against it
- Pray in the Spirit an hour a day
- Fast as the Lord leads you.
- Pray and select some Scriptures to declare against it.

Chapter 4

Dealing with Death

- Are you grieving over someone's death?
- Are you angry with God?
- Was your faith shattered?
- Have you given up on prayer as a result of your hurt and disappointment?

What you do now is very important. If you answered "yes" to any of the above questions, you could be stuck in your walk with God. You may be stranded somewhere without the ability to move forward. In order to get over it, there are a few things that you must do.

My Story

I was a teenager when my great-grandmother died. It was my first time dealing with the death of a family member. She was old and although I was upset with the way they prepared her for viewing, it wasn't hard to deal with.

The next death I had to deal with was my father-in-law. I was 19 years old and my husband was in Vietnam. My father-in-law was someone that I knew loved me. He had hand-picked me to meet his son and was thrilled when we got married. I married Nick hoping he would turn out just like his dad. Because he quit taking his blood pressure medicine, my father-in-law suddenly was in critical condition due to a cerebral hemorrhage. This was overwhelming. Within 24 hours someone that I knew loved me was suddenly gone. I cried and cried. I made a few trips to the cemetery and was depressed after I went each time. After time went by, I was okay.

I became a Christian about five years later and then it was over 20 years before I faced death again. I had learned about the power of prayer. I had heard that whatever we ask in prayer, believing, we would receive. I had been taught that faith would move mountains. These teachings were all based on Scriptures that Jesus had spoken. One thing not taught to me was the sovereignty of God. That word is a big word that means: God is the one who is in control and decides.

My friend Emily had cancer. We had known each other for years and our children were friends. She was 39 years old and we found out later that she had ignored symptoms for a long time. When she finally went to the doctor, the prognosis was not good. I prayed. The church prayed. We believed she would be healed. Doctors performed heroic measures. She had chemotherapy and radiation. Quite a bit of time passed.

Emily's unsaved husband and all of us were shattered when she died leaving three children behind. In my mind I could accept my grandmother's death because she was old. My father-in-law had not taken his blood pressure problem seriously and died as a result of it. But this was different. We were Christians, praying for another Christian, according to the Word of God, and she died. This was a serious blow to my faith and my relationship with God.

My mind began to question the Bible – even God. "Lord, I stood on Your promises. Where were You?" I seriously doubted that I could ever pray again for someone to be healed. I did not understand. I worked through this sometime later with the Lord and my mind was changed in how I view death.

It was during the next year that I had a session with the Lord that dealt with my disappointment. My perspective on death changed and I began to trust God in a new way.

A few years later, I got the word that Kimberly had died. Kimberly was a young mother and it was hard to believe that it had been three years since she was diagnosed with leukemia. She had a son that was five years old at the time of her death. She had stood in faith believing for her healing. Our church had stood with her, many of us making trips to visit her as she had her treatments out of town. Again, we had prayed and asked for the Lord to heal someone and they had died. My reaction this time was different.

I prayed this prayer when I heard about Kimberly's death:

"Lord, I pray for Your people, who are being shaken by this perceived tragedy of Kimberly's death. Lord, she is now in that great crowd of witnesses that is cheering us onward and upward. She has slipped from this world into the one she was created for. She is forever free of pain, suffering, rejection, and disease and those things that hurt her while she was here. Comfort us who are left behind and let us not be damaged by not understanding 'why' and let us not shrink back from You, the only one who can give us peace. We pray for her child to be comforted and that You will give someone to nurture him. We will see her again."

Following is my paraphrase taken from the Amplified Bible:

I wouldn't want you ignorant about those who have died that you may not grieve for them like the unsaved people who have no hope beyond the grave. We believe that Jesus died and rose again, even so God will bring with Him through Jesus those who have fallen asleep in death. For the Lord Himself will descend from heaven with a shout. There will be a trumpet blast and those who have departed this life will rise first, then we, the living, shall be caught up in the clouds to meet Him and we shall throughout all eternity be with the Lord! Therefore comfort and encourage one another with these words. (1 Thessalonians 4:13-18)

It was only a short time after Kimberly died and I had written the previous words that death struck closer to home. My grandson, Jordan, was eleven years old. He and his best friend were having target practice and a gun went off when the barrel was accidentally bumped. The bullet ricocheted through the trees and went into Jordan striking his aorta, the main artery of the body. Doctors performed dramatic efforts to save Jordan's life, but there was not anything humanly possible that could be done. Cries went up to God on his behalf. Finally that evening, the laboring by doctors ceased. Jordan was gone. A shocked and stunned family didn't know what to do. The first decision we made was to not blame God. If we had not chosen this stance, it would have been impossible to receive the peace and comfort of the Holy Spirit. We miss Jordan, and it took time, but we healed.

Our Family Has Experienced Many Close Calls with Death

My Husband's Story

As a teenager, my husband was diving off a houseboat with his friends. Something was wrong on this last dive for when he came to the surface, he was underneath the hull of the boat. He made a right turn and swam and tried to surface. He was still under the boat. He repeated the strategy of turning and swimming and attempted to emerge from the murky Bay water, and could not. With his lungs desperate for air, he finally made it to the surface. He could have drowned that day.

My Story

My sister and I were teenagers on family vacation. We did not realize that the Atlantic Ocean was slowly gaining control over us. We were oblivious to the darkening sky. It was Jacksonville Beach in the late 60s and our idea of fun was riding air rafts on the waves. To begin with, we floated in the slow rolling waves doing the usual kid-stuff of tipping each other over. And on that last day of vacation, we were excited that finally some bigger surf was kicking up. Our only concern was being propelled through the shallows and burning our knees by the friction of the sand. Wow, what a blast!

The rip tide was carrying us further and further from shore. In a short passage of time our circumstances changed from playing in the surf near the beach, to being caught in waves that only allowed us to grab a frantic breath before the next one crashed on us. A storm was brewing and no matter how hard we tried, we were stuck right where we were.

A siren went off and people gathered along the shore. My sister's raft was ripped from her grasp by a huge wave. I grabbed her and we both clung desperately to mine.

I don't know why we are stuck in these waves, I thought to myself. *It must be because of this stupid raft, and at this rate we'll never get to shore!*

Filling my lungs with air, I let go and made a lunge toward the beach, kicking furiously with my feet and pulling hard with my arms. My sister grasped me by the ankle and held tightly so I gave up and went back to clinging to the raft with her. She must have thought I lost my grip and there was no way to explain to her what I was doing. As we gasped for air between crashing waves, I saw a swimmer plowing through the surf, coming toward us. It was a lifeguard with a small oblong float. One end had a rope which was slung over his shoulder and at the other end there was a loop he wanted us to grab. I certainly did not want to release the raft which I knew could keep my head above water, but he yelled, "Grab this and let it go!" We followed his orders and he plowed right back through the surf to the shore, towing us as he swam.

As the family gathered around us, we learned that our father had attempted to come to our rescue and both he and another lifeguard were rescued by boat because they were caught in the undertow. Where had our lifeguard come from and where did he go? Hmmm. He was not in the detailed report published in the *Jacksonville Beach News*.

Thirty-one years later when I was telling the story to my children, my sister overheard me and corrected part of the story.

She said, "I never grabbed hold of your ankle. I was holding on for dear life!"

It was then that I realized that God had saved my life that day. Not just through humans, but with supernatural help. He had grabbed me by the ankle and it could have been an angel that rescued us.

Twice in recent years, one of my children was riding with me in a car and suddenly a car was headed straight toward us in our lane about to hit us head-on. In a flash of time, without losing control of our vehicle, we were off the road and stopped, and the oncoming car was still in our lane as it passed us. These could have been head-on collisions that were miraculously prevented. All these incidents have come back to mind. As our family reflected on these near-tragic events from the past, we realized that we, His people, are on this earth to fulfill our destiny. Over and over God has intervened to see that we don't exit this life too soon. Much of His intervention even took place before we gave our lives to Him. With this in mind, we must trust that He knows the particular destiny He has for each individual and He knows when "exit" time has come.

Knowing that we are His and that He is in control has brought me to a new level of trusting Him that I never knew existed. And though life on this earth has joys *and* sorrows, I choose to trust the wisdom and timing of God and to receive His grace for whatever comes my way. My whole perspective on life has been changed. The words in the Scriptures have come alive! They were written with *eternity* being the focus.

It is evident that God goes to much trouble to keep us here. We need to trust and accept when He lets someone go.

The Power of Choice

I had to choose to accept God's choice to take my grandson to be with Him. I chose to believe that regardless of how I felt, God was in control. Our friend, Ted, gave us this verse, *Your eyes saw my unformed body. All the days ordained for me were written in Your book before one of them came to be.* (Psalm 139:16 NIV)

In the first days of my daughter grieving over her loss, the Lord gave her a vision of Jordan and he came to her in the night. She felt his presence and could see a faint outline of him. He said, "Hey, Mom!" She told him she loved him and he was gone. It was then that she received an amazing peace and got her first full night's sleep. Jordan is alive! This made life beyond this one more real!

One of my daughters, who was very close to Jordan, has had several dreams with him talking to her about what heaven is like. Our perspective has changed.

So I ask you again, are you grieving over someone's death? Are you angry with God? Was your faith shattered? Have you given up on prayer as a result of your hurt and disappointment? You can get over it.

What You Must Do

- Forgiveness: You need to forgive the drunk driver of the car, or the doctor who made an error, or the person who was responsible in some other way for the death of the one you loved. You may even blame yourself. If it was by a disease or a so-called "act of God" such as lightning, hurricane, or boat sinking or if you feel like God *could* have prevented the other tragic way it happened, you must forgive God also. So forgive God and man. Just reading this may cause feelings of anger to surface and you could be thinking, *How could I ever forgive?* It is a choice that you must make. God's Word says that if we don't forgive others, He will not forgive us. If you have prayed the Lord's Prayer, you have repeated the words, "and forgive us out trespasses (sins) *as* we forgive those who have trespassed against us."

- Check your emotions: It is possible that you cannot forgive. You can pray right now for the Lord to *help* you to forgive. Pray this simple prayer: "Help me forgive, Lord."

- Then pray: Lord, I choose by an act of my will to forgive _____ (fill in the names) for everything they did (add if it applies) and for everything they didn't do that they should have done. Lord, I choose by an act of my will to forgive You for allowing this and for _____. Now I forgive myself completely for (let go of regrets) _____
_____.

- Restoration: In order for the pain in your heart to end, you need healing. Pray this prayer: Lord, heal me. Heal my disappointment in life and my disappointment in people. Heal my disappointment in You. I ask You to heal my broken heart. Thank You for doing these things and for taking away my grief and pain. In Jesus name, amen.

Chapter 5

Deceived! You're Always the Last to Know

Our Story

Bahamas, here we come! It had long been my husband's dream to live on a boat in the Caribbean. He had a vision of helping the remote islands develop ports using his thirty years of experience in heavy construction. Times had been tough on his business in the recession, and we reached a decision. If we were going to struggle with finances, we might as well do something with purpose. We decided to sell off the equipment that was left in his construction company and launch out on our journey to fulfill this dream. The entire family was in one accord.

We ordered books and began homeschooling our children. All the Christmas gifts that year were strictly oriented to boat life. We got slickers (foul weather gear), color coded towels and wash cloths and glasses for the kitchen that were unbreakable.

We had lots of stuff that we had accumulated in a four-bedroom house, and we began the process of paring down. With a garage sale we ridded ourselves of file cabinets, office furniture, and household items. We prayed about what to do with our furnishings and made out a list of what few things we wanted to put in storage and how to dispose of the rest. When our crane sold for $13,000, we decided it was time to take the leap!

As we left Panama City pulling a U-Haul behind our van in March 1986, our pastor prayed over us and blessed us. We wept with church-family members at that last service. It was an exciting and scary time, but we truly felt that God was with us. Our journey took us to Key West and then on to Hope Town, Abaco, Bahamas. Within ten days we had located a boat that had been seized by Customs. A vessel left in their waters for over six months at a time was considered imported. So because the import duty was assessed, it was abandoned by the American owners. It was worth approximately $100,000, and we decided to make a formal bid on it. After praying, we felt led to offer a bid to the Bahamian government for $7,000 and we returned to the U.S. We were told it would be a while before they would have an answer on our bid.

My father lived in Tampa, so we picked that location. Within a few days, my husband had gone to work for a marine construction company in that area, been given a new company vehicle, and a great salary. We were so grateful for the Lord's provision! We signed a short-term apartment lease and I continued homeschooling our children. Our children who were ages sixteen and ten were very motivated in their studies and didn't require any instruction. Our eight year old son was the only one I actually had to teach. Our pre-schooler was three. We were drawing very close as a family.

After a few months, we received a telegram that we had been awarded the boat! We had a very short period of time to act or the deal would be canceled. The only problem was, we no longer had the money to buy it. We prayed. We called our pastor back in Panama City, Florida and he offered to lend us the money to purchase the boat. My husband told him, "If this is God's idea, He will supply the money for the boat." Later that evening, the phone rang and it was someone in Alabama who had heard of our step of faith from someone back at our home church. It was amazing to talk to a couple who had so much in common with us. The couple was exactly the same age as we were and felt called to go to the Islands also. Their idea had to do with working with missionaries in the area and trans-porting people and goods between the islands, and they were even using the same curriculum to homeschool their children. We shared about the boat, and didn't expect to hear from them again.

An hour later, the phone rang. It was the couple that had called earlier. Clark said, "We think we know someone who will buy you the boat!" There was a man in their city that had a very prosperous business. Actually, there were two brothers who were in partner-ship. They had become Christians and one went to the mission field and the other felt his call was to continue in business and support missions. The only catch would be that the boat would be in his company name so that he could be accountable tax-wise. We talked it over and my husband said, "If this is the Lord, it doesn't matter whose name the boat is in." It was "a done deal." My husband notified his employer that this had come together for us and let him know he would not be with the company for long. His boss said he would begin to seek a replacement but that he was welcome to stay with the company until that time.

The $7,000 was wired to us to pay for the boat and it was arranged that as we made repairs, we would keep our receipts and mail them for reimbursement. The "donor" was to remain anonymous. All we had was the company name that the boat would be assigned to. Months went by and clean up and repairs to the vessel were made and a number of trips were made to the Bahamas. We were reimbursed for the expenses.

My husband and I had met Clark and his family personally by this time and we shared testimonies of how we all came to the Lord. It was a good time of fellowship in the moonlight on a dock on the east coast of Florida. Soon after, my husband and oldest son flew with Clark and his two sons down to the Bahamas to bring the boat back to the States.

Time passed. It was around Thanksgiving of that year when we sent off the second batch of receipts totaling $5,000 by Registered Mail for reimbursement. After a few weeks, we received our letter back. It had never been picked up even after several notices had been served. We felt like there had to be some mistake so we attempted to call Clark. We spoke with his wife and she was very vague with us. Our short-term lease on the apartment was up December 31 and we had several things happen at once. My husband's employer said he had found his replacement and gave him two-week's notice. I had done my best to locate another short-term lease and had not been successful. We didn't know what to do, so I packed up the van and returned to Panama City when the last day of December arrived. My husband stayed with my father the last days of his job and then returned to Panama City.

We all "camped out" at my in-laws' home to try to sort out what to do. I thought, *Wow, was our not being able to find an apartment and the job ending, a sign from the Lord that we were to move over to the east coast and work full-time on the vessel to get it in shape?*

My husband made a phone call to a businessman he knew in the same city where Clark and the donor lived in. "John," he said, "Is it possible for you to find out who the corporate officers are in an organization in your city?" "Sure, give me the company name," he replied. "I'll call you back." Later that day, we were stunned to find that Clark, our "partner" had deceived us and *he* was the owner of our boat.

It took some time to process the discovery in my mind. This couldn't be happening to us! When My husband confronted Clark on the phone, he offered to sell us the boat for $30,000 – over four times what he paid for it and was not willing to reimburse us for the $5,000 we spent on repairs. There was nothing we could do to get our money back.

By this time, our family of six had temporarily moved into our pastor's beach house. My husband walked over to the fireplace and burned the receipts and said, "I shake the dust off of my shoes." I thought this was very mature of him but I wanted to scream! I was angry and struggled to be able to forgive someone who would do this to us.

My husband found another job in south Florida and we relocated and journeyed forward into what turned out to be a series of disappointments for him. Promises were made by employers and not kept. There was a period of nine months before we moved back to Panama City that we did not even have a home. We stayed with friends and family, homeschooled and traveled. The summer of 1986 we borrowed money to set up housekeeping again. We went bargain hunting and found a $35 couch, slept on a mattress on the floor, bought clothing at the consignment store, and used a Laundromat since I had given away the washer and dryer. My husband set out to find contracting work again. The children were awarded scholarships at the Christian school they had attended before. We came back to our church and people could hardly believe that Christians had "ripped us off."

It took a few years before we realized what had happened to us. First of all, we thought that God was leading us in this venture. We had many false confirmations along the way. And, although work in the Bahama Islands could be part of my husband's call in ministry/ business, it would be far into the future. I drew consolation from the

Scriptures. Moses knew that the Lord had called him to be a deliverer for the Israelites, took matters in his own hands and then ran for his life. He spent forty years on the back side of the desert being prepared for his call. Then the time came for him to do what God prepared him to do.

Bottom line: We were deceived. The whole thing should never have happened. We lost two years, had to start completely over. One of our daughters asked, "Are we nomads?"

In review, these are the steps that were taken to lead us into deception:

1. Groundwork was laid. The enemy strategized based on our obvious flaws in regard to accountability and authority. We were operating independently of the Body of Christ. The Lord has set up checks and balances for us if we will avail ourselves to them. God has placed people in leadership positions in the Body of Christ. Not being open to receiving counsel, we never asked anyone what they thought or asked them to pray for us about it. The Scriptures say, *Where there is no counsel, the people fall; but in the multitude of counselors there is safety.* (Proverbs 11:14 NKJ) *Without counsel, plans go awry, but in the multitude of counselors they are established.* (Proverbs 15:22 NKJ) We had not sought the counsel of leaders.

2. We ignored the warnings. It isn't the Lord's will that we stray off into error. Many times, we can look back and remember a "gut" feeling we had and ignored. Other times there were obvious signs that we disregarded. For instance our oldest daughter had given us a book titled, *Is That Really You God?*, by Loren Cunningham, founder of Youth With A Mission. In the book he tells about being deceived regarding acquiring a ship for the ministry. The book so paralleled our story, it is hard to believe we missed the warning. Also, I can't believe we missed this one: the name of the boat we found in the Bahamas was "*Arrogance*"!

3. The enemy knows how we are looking for confirmations and will go to great lengths to be sure we keep heading in the wrong direction. We received false confirmations which kept us confident that God was leading us.

There are many born-again Christians being deceived. The word deceive means to beguile, to make a person believe what is not true, to mislead, or to cause to err. (Encarta) God warns His people, Israel, in the Old Testament about deception. And we, as New Testament believers, are warned in the Word about it also. Ignorance is a key weapon used by our adversary. Satan is the master of deception, which is delusion and trickery.

Being ignorant of God's ways is the basic problem. Because we do not understand how the Lord set up His government in the Body of Christ and the purpose for it, we are easily sabotaged. We also do not take the Word of God to heart. We are instructed to be a doer of the Word and not a hearer only. This failure on our part can become more and more evident as the schemes of the enemy are played out in our lives.

How Does Deception Work Against Christians?

One of the names for Christians is "believers." There is an outright war against our faith to cause us not to believe.

The main purpose of deception is to get a person off track. Another intention is to sabotage our faith. The enemy likes for us to stick our faith way out there and have it dashed on the rocks so that when God really has something for us to do, we will hang back to protect ourselves just in case it is not the Lord.

Here are some guidelines I discovered in hearing from the Lord. We need to have the answer to the question, "Is that really You, God?"

- The basic guideline is: Does it line up with the Word of God? It must agree with the over-all principles revealed in Scriptures and with the nature of God. If a person does not have a general knowledge of the Lord as revealed through the Scriptures, he or she could be an easy target for deception.

- Another vital thing is our relationship with the Lord. We need to have daily fellowship and communication with the

Lord and learn to hear His voice. However, even then it is possible that we can miss hearing correctly. Always confirm that you are hearing correctly when making major decisions.

- Realize that your hearing is not perfect. We may have a tendency to "fill in the blanks" or second-guess what the Lord would have us to do and then we take it as direction from the Lord.

- We must learn to recognize when it is not God that has spoken to us. It can be quite painful to discover. Years later people still ask, "Didn't you live on a boat in the Bahamas?"

- Sometimes, what we thought God was going to do, He did not do and we've made a fool out of ourselves or we gave money at what we perceived was His direction and we lost it.

Years ago, there was teaching that went around that gave us permission to ask boldly for things and we just knew God would answer. It was a distortion of Scriptures and it produced a "hyper"-faith that did not originate with God. This resulted in doing drastic things that we thought were in obedience to the Lord. We had heard that "without faith it is impossible to please God," so we stuck our faith *way* out there. We did this numerous times and finally ended up in a spiritual ditch and threw the "faith message" out the window. This was all a deliberate attempt by the enemy to ruin that area of our Christian walk so that we would get into unbelief.

We also have much teaching and human experience that could cause us to be deceived into thinking that God is not pleased with us if we don't take these steps of faith. We must really know Him. The time invested in the daily relationship is what will get us back on track when we have second-guessed the Lord and messed up.

When we start down a path, and feel that something is not right, we can go to Him and say, if this is really You asking me to do this, I must know beyond a shadow of a doubt – yes or no. We must be willing to take "no" for an answer and humble ourselves and get in a position to even hear correction. Seeking godly counsel from a trusted leader may also be necessary. I truly believe that we can learn from every mistake and let what we learn become more of our armor to protect us from deception the next time.

Several people I know have been deceived. The deceived person is usually the last to know. With different individuals, I fasted and prayed before confronting them with what the Lord showed me regarding the deception. Their eyes were opened to see that they had been misled. It was humbling and painful for them to make this discovery.

The thoughts that accompany deception are that we would be in unbelief if we didn't continue on in faith. We feel we must proceed onward regardless of our feelings. It feels like God is in it because there is a struggle of faith – which is not to be moved by what our eyes see and to keep believing because our faith is being tested.

How do we tell if it is God speaking to us or we are being deceived? A real key is to humble ourselves and seek godly counsel.

Have You Ever Been Deceived?

Prayer: Lord, heal the damage that was done to me as a result of being deceived. I forgive myself for being fooled by the enemy. Restore my faith that has been hindered as a result of this. I forgive You, God, if I have blamed You in any way. Help me to apply Your principles to my life and to become accountable to spiritual authority in the Body of Christ. I'm not sure I understand how this works, but I am willing to learn. In Jesus name I pray. Amen.

Chapter 6

Forgiveness

*M*any people have a problem with forgiveness. It doesn't appear to be a problem because it's not a conscious thing. We all have been disappointed by people. There are those who reject, criticize, and hurt us. Sometimes we are the recipient of a vicious, cruel act. Things happen that can never be un-done. When we feel victimized by others, we make the decision "I will never forgive them for that!" That seems like a good way to punish the perpetrator. That may be the world's way of punishment, but it is not God's way. What has just taken place is another inner vow. And the vow has power over us until we give it up. Unforgiveness doesn't affect the other person, but can affect the person holding unforgiveness spiritually and even physically.

The blood of Jesus has cleansed all of us who have received Him as our Lord and Savior. It cleansed us from the power of sin and the penalty of sin: past, present, and future. We need to appropriate all that the Lord has provided for us. We can experience wonderful freedom if we will do what He said in Mark 11:25 (NKJ): *And whenever you stand praying, if you have anything against anyone, forgive him, that your Father in heaven may also forgive you your sins.*

Be merciful, just as your Father is merciful. Do not judge, and you will not be judged. Do not condemn, and you will not be condemned. Forgive, and you will be forgiven. Give, and it will be given to you. A good measure, pressed down, shaken together and running over, will be poured into your lap. For with the measure you use, it will be measured to you. (Luke 6:36-38 NIV)

When we have forgiven someone we no longer talk about what they did to us. If we are still talking about it and reliving it, then we are giving the enemy permission to torment us. In Matthew 18, Jesus shares a parable of the servant who would not forgive someone else's small financial debt after he had been released from a huge debt. The servant's master grew angry and turned him over to the jailers to have him tormented until he paid back his debt. Jesus said, *This is how my heavenly Father will treat each of you unless you forgive your brother from your heart.* (Matthew 18:35 NIV)

Forgiveness from God is complete and total and He expects nothing less from us.

Who is a God like You, who pardons sin and forgives the transgression of the remnant of His inheritance? You do not stay angry forever but delight to show mercy. You will again have compassion on us; You will tread our sins underfoot and hurl all our iniquities into the depths of the sea. (Micah 7:18-19 NIV)

It is obvious that forgiveness is not an option if we plan to obey the Lord. Disobedience leaves a door open to satan. The enemy also has access into our lives through the wounds we experience. If we forgive and ask the Lord to heal us, the enemy loses his power in that area. If we become bitter and unforgiving, our wounds fester and the enemy torments us with pain. We relive what was done to us or get poked by someone else along the way, and our wounds go deeper and deeper. We have a choice. Each of us was given a free will and we need to use it. The choice is whether to hang on to the past through unforgiveness and continue a life of torment or to make the decision to forgive because the Lord commands it. Remember forgiveness is a choice, not a feeling.

Getting over the past is really a two-part process. Forgiveness is one part and having the Lord heal us is the other. Years ago, I only knew about the first part. I forgave any and all people who hurt, offended, and disappointed me. But I found that one person in particular could ruin my day in just a moment! I was moody at times and didn't know why. I discovered that the pain was still there. That is when I realized there were two sides to this. I prayed and told the Lord how each thing had hurt me and asked for healing. He did it! In God's Kingdom, everything we receive from the Lord is through faith and this healing of the soul and emotional realm is no different. Will you make the choice to get over the past?

Prayer: Lord, I ask You to help me. I receive Your grace to face these hurts and to forgive each and every person. Holy Spirit, I ask You to bring people to my mind that I need to forgive.

My Story

In the fourth grade, a classmate had speckled me with black paint while we worked on the bulletin board together in the hall. When I entered the classroom, I asked the teacher if I could go and wash my hands. She turned to the class and said, "Well, look who's here, *Messy Bessy!* The whole class laughed and I felt embarrassed and humiliated. Even as an adult, I had a fear of being humiliated again. I prayed like this, "Lord, I forgive Mrs. Johnson for what she did to me so long ago. Heal me of the damage that was done to me."

When the people begin to come to your mind, say, "Lord, I choose to forgive (say their name). I ask You to heal me." Continue as long as names and incidents come to your mind. Then, when you feel you are finished, thank the Lord for helping you to do this. Then pray, "I close the door to the enemy and any bondage that came into my life as result of these incidents, I command to be broken and gone in Jesus name. Amen!"

Beyond Forgiveness

My Story

Living in the panhandle of Florida caused excitement that year as major storms developed. The Weather Channel kept us informed and this time it looked quite possible our lives would be interrupted. We did everything possible to prepare for loss of power or water. We stocked our pantry, bought batteries, and cooked up lots of food and froze it.

"If a hurricane is going to hit our area, this might be our last chance to have some air conditioned 'girl time.' Let's go out for dessert and coffee!"

"Sounds good to me," my daughter said, as she shut down her computer. "Office work can wait."

As we drove to the restaurant, we talked about our friends in south Florida that had been without power and air conditioning for two weeks following an earlier storm that summer. The current predictions had put us in the possible strike zone.

As the hostess led us to our table, someone that I had known years ago called my name and rushed up and hugged me. We began to talk about the approaching hurricane. Her condo on the beach had been totally wiped out by a hurricane ten years previously. She shared how she had feared that it would happen again and then how God assured her that all would be well after the storm passed. I smiled and said, "That's great." Then I slid into the booth with my daughter.

This person had wounded me very deeply years ago. In keeping with my habit of choosing to forgive, this had been dealt with and eventually healing was a reality for me. Because of this, there were no old feelings stirred up when I saw her. There was not even a twinge. My daughter and I went on to have our tiramisu and coffee and enjoyed our time together.

Later, that day I thought more about the encounter. I realized that although I did not want the hurricane to demolish her present house, I did not *care* if it did. Uh oh! I realized that something was wrong with that picture! I am a Christian and she is a Christian. I should not be void of concern for her. I thought about what Jesus said, "Bless those who persecute you and say all manner of evil against you." I remembered that Stephen prayed, "Forgive them" when people were stoning him to death and Jesus prayed to His Father for those who were crucifying Him, "Father, forgive them..." So I immediately began to pray for her peace. Her new home was in an area that would have a mandatory evacuation. In prayer, I blessed her and prayed for protection of everything that belonged to her. During this time I did not *feel* anything. I was just obeying what I felt the Lord was leading me to do. Afterward, I sensed that something tangible had happened in my heart. I cared! This is what love does. It goes beyond the command to forgive and goes the extra mile to make a choice to act in love by blessing the person. Perhaps there is someone you have forgiven but you could use a change of heart toward them.

Prayer: I choose once again to forgive _____ for everything they ever said or did in the past and I ask You to bless them, bless their family, and all that belongs to them, in Jesus name. Amen.

Chapter 7

How to Overcome Anger

*O*vercoming anger is a choice. Unless someone really wants to let go of their anger, he or she will not do it. It is their way of punishing the one who has offended or hurt them.

My Story

It happened in a restaurant. I was casually eating my meal and talking with someone whom I had known for years and years. Our conversation turned to a sensitive subject and she made a sarcastic, opinionated remark about one of my family members. It triggered a reaction and a flash of rage went through me. It was a power that I had never experienced before and it startled me. No words came out of my mouth. It was all internal. Something that wasn't *me* took over for a moment. I had always been able to control my emotions and this was a sign that it wasn't working! Then I knew what those people on death row were talking about: "I don't know what came over me!"

Have you ever seen something boil over on the stove? I found out that people have a boiling-over point too! I could simmer and then cool off, but when rage showed up, I was shocked at the feelings. Later as I was thinking back over what happened, I asked myself, "Why did I react so strongly?" I tried to justify my reaction and blame the other person for it. I had a "history" with this person and there were some unresolved issues, and the comment she made to me caused the boiling-over point! I had been grumbling inside myself for a while about the way this person related to me.

In my time with the Lord, I asked, "Why am I so angry?" Strong impressions and feelings came to my mind. I remembered how I dreaded confrontation and that was why I let things build up instead of dealing with them. I found out there was a way to get rid of anger. It began by being honest with myself and with God. I had to identify the root cause. If there are weeds growing in our yard or garden, we can cut them down and it looks like they are gone. But, they will grow back unless we dig them up by the roots. We don't just want to control our emotions so we act better. We want to find out what the root cause of anger is so we can dig it up and get it out.

If we don't deal with the root cause, we cannot get rid of it. Most of the time the root cause is that we have been hurt. It may be because of being abused either with words or by something that was done to us. Sometimes an adult takes advantage of a child. We can be angry over circumstances that we have no power to control. There are lots of reasons to be angry, but God says:

Refrain from anger and turn from wrath; do not fret – it leads only to evil. (Psalm 37:8 NIV)

Let all bitterness, wrath, anger, clamor, and evil speaking be put away from you, with all malice. And be kind to one another, tenderhearted, forgiving one another, just as God in Christ also forgave you. (Ephesians 4:31-32 NKJ)

If we want to grow as a Christian, we must receive the truth and apply it to our life. The Scriptures reveal how God feels about us holding on to anger. Even though it feels more comfortable to hold on to it, we *must* let it go.

After the restaurant experience, it was like a bomb was about to go off inside me. I wondered how to de-fuse it. I said to the Lord, "Give me some keys and I'll use them and teach others how to do the same."

The following keys were given to me as I spent time with the Lord, praying and listening. They were completely effective.

Four Keys to Dealing with Anger

Key #1: Be Honest With Yourself and God

Get paper and pen and ask God to show you the first time you remember being angry in your life. Why were you angry? What happened to you? Ask the Lord to help you face whatever it is. There may be many issues that come up and perhaps it will take some time to search your heart and write down things to pray about. Once you identify the root cause(s) of your anger, there is something else you must do. We will use the Bible as our guide.

Key #2: Healing

You may have tried to forgive others but it didn't last because the hurt needed to be healed.

Read Psalm 23 as a prayer:

*The Lord is my shepherd; I shall not want. He makes me to lie down in green pastures; He leads me beside the still waters. **He restores my soul**; He leads me in the paths of righteousness for His name's sake. Yea, though I walk through the valley of the shadow of death, I will fear no evil; for You are with me; Your rod and Your staff, they comfort me. You prepare a table before me in the presence of my enemies; You* *anoint my head with oil; My cup runs over. Surely goodness and mercy shall follow me; All the days of my life; And I will dwell in the house of the Lord Forever.* (NKJV)

Prayer for inner healing:

Place your hand over your heart and pray –

Lord, heal any damage that was done to me through the things I have gone through. I thank You for healing every hurting place in me and restoring my soul.

Key #3: Forgiving and Repenting

What does Jesus have to say about forgiveness? In the Lord's Prayer: *Our Father in heaven, hallowed be Your name, Your kingdom come, Your will be done on earth as it is in heaven. Give us today our daily bread.* ***Forgive us our debts, as we also have forgiven our debtors****. And lead us not into temptation, but deliver us from the evil one. For if you forgive men when they sin against you, your heavenly Father will also forgive you, but if you do not forgive men their sins, your Father will not forgive your sins.* (Matthew 6:9-15 NIV)

Then Peter came to Him and said, "Lord, how often shall my brother sin against me, and I forgive him? Up to seven times?" Jesus said to him, "I do not say to you, up to seven times, but up to seventy times seven. Therefore the kingdom of heaven is like a certain king who wanted to settle accounts with his servants. And when he had begun to settle accounts, one was brought to him who owed him ten thousand talents. But as he was not able to pay, his master commanded that he be sold, with his wife and children and all that he had, and that payment be made. The servant therefore fell down before him, saying, 'Master, have patience with me, and I will pay you all.' Then the master of that servant was moved with compassion, released him, and forgave him the debt. But that servant went out and found one of his fellow servants who owed him a hundred denarii; and he laid hands on him and took him by the throat, saying, 'Pay me what you owe!' So his fellow servant fell down at his feet and begged him, saying, 'Have patience with me, and I will pay you all.' And he would not, but went and threw him into prison till he should pay the debt. So when his fellow servants saw what had been done, they were very grieved, and came and told their master all that had been done. Then his master, after he had called him, said to him, 'You wicked servant! I forgave you all that debt because you begged me. Should you not also have had compassion on your fellow servant, just as I had pity on you?' And his master was angry, and delivered him to the torturers until he should pay all that was due to him. So My heavenly Father also will do to you if each of you,

from his heart, does not forgive his brother his trespasses."
(Matthew 18:21-35 NKJ)

Forgiveness is a choice – not a feeling. If you do not feel like you can do it, stop and ask the Lord for the grace to forgive from the heart. He will certainly help you carry out His will! Then pray a prayer like this:

Lord, I want to be set free from anger. In obedience to You, I choose by an act of my will to forgive _____
for everything they have done against me.

Proceed this way until you have forgiven all those who come to your mind. (Be as specific as you need to in order to be sure you are really dealing with the root.)

Repent for your own actions and reactions.

Lord, You paid the price for all my sins and wiped my slate clean. Because of my hurt, I did not show mercy to others like You showed to me. I repent for holding all this against them and for_____. (Be specific about what you have done to retaliate in words and actions.)

Key # 4: Deliverance

Prayer for deliverance: Lord, help me break my old habit patterns and reactions. I am willing to change. I renounce unforgiveness, anger, wrath, rage, revenge, retaliation, violence and murder. I command them to leave my life now!

Declaration: I choose to be kind to others, tenderhearted, forgiving others, even as God for Christ's sake has forgiven me. As one of God's chosen people, I am holy and dearly loved and choose to clothe myself with compassion, kindness, humility, gentleness and patience. I will bear with others and forgive whatever grievances I may have against them. I will forgive as the Lord forgave me. I'm putting on love and will let the peace of God rule in my heart! (Based on Colossians 3:12-15 NIV and Ephesians 4:32 NKJ.)

This declaration needs to be spoken every day until the truth of it is in your heart. Then, when you are tempted to hold on to an offense, you can speak it to yourself, choose to forgive, and ask the Lord to heal your hurt or disappointment. Choices like this will cause you to be victorious over the enemy!

After I had been healed and delivered from the anger and rage, I became very conscious of choices I made after that. The memory of what had been done to me flashed back in my mind while driving down the road. There was the opportunity to rehearse and relive what I got set free from. By choosing not to do it, the thoughts faded away.

The next day, I got mad again. I realize then that it was a habit. When I caught myself grumbling about other drivers I stopped myself. Anger is an emotion. We have to learn not to be ruled by our emotions.

In order to be angry and not sin, the offense needs to be dealt with that day or else it will grow and progress to worse levels. There is a Biblical example of the first instance of anger in the story of Cain and Abel in Genesis 4.

So the LORD *said to Cain, "Why are you angry? And why has your countenance fallen? If you do well, will you not be accepted? And if you do not do well, sin lies at the door. And its desire is for you, but you should rule over it." Now Cain talked with Abel his brother; and it came to pass, when they were in the field, that Cain rose up against Abel his brother and killed him.* (Genesis 4:6-8 NKJ)

God asked the question, "Why are you angry?" Even though God knows everything, it is for us that He asks so that we will be honest with Him and ourselves. There is a choice. *Sin is crouching at the door [...] you* **must** *master it.* (Genesis 4:7 NASB) The anger is not the sin. It is what we do with the anger. Later Cain lied to God when asked where his brother was. He said, "I don't know." Then he made a sarcastic and angry remark, "Am I my brother's keeper?" God asked him another question, "What have you done?" Cain didn't answer. (Genesis 4:9-10 NIV)

Anger is one of the things the enemy uses to steal, kill, and destroy. We must not tolerate it in our lives!

Chapter 8

False Responsibilities

My Story

For Mother's Day I received some plants from one of my children. Among them were cherry tomato plants.

"Oooh, fresh tomatoes!" I said to myself.

I potted the plants and put them on my back porch and they were looking good! I had no idea what a project they would turn out to be. They must be watered every day and fertilized regularly.

"Oh no! What in the world are these little green worm-like creatures in all sizes? They are eating the leaves and my tiny green tomatoes before they even have a chance to reach maturity."

Off to the store I went. "Sevin® dust is what you need," instructed the lady in the garden center. So I came back home and sprinkled the dust over the plants to kill the pesky critters. It worked.

"Oh my goodness! Now there are little holes in my tomatoes. The birds are ruining them."

My husband came to the rescue and constructed a system with netting to protect my plants from the birds.

This went on for weeks.

"Now the tomatoes look too small. Oops, I've forgotten to fertilize. Must remedy that. No, I think I will throw the plants into the ditch behind our house and say, forget it! Who needs this trouble? I can buy cherry tomatoes at the grocery store!"

This is what it is like to take on false responsibility. Sometimes we end up doing this kind of thing just because we are qualified, available, and able to take it on. It could develop into a huge amount of trouble, distracting us from things that have real purpose.

Taking on false responsibilities has been one of my biggest problems. We are responsible to walk out our salvation with fear and trembling and to cast all our cares on the Lord because He cares for us. We are to pray without ceasing and to love the Lord with all our heart, soul, mind and strength. We are responsible to fear the Lord and turn from evil. We are to pursue love – get the picture? We are not to worry about people and things, worry about "what if?" or try to figure things out. There is a big difference between responsibility and false responsibility. For instance, we are to love people, but that does not require us to give them what they demand from us or even *sweetly* ask from us.

It is easy to take up burdens that are not ours to carry. When we do that we neglect what is ours. This is a deliberate strategy from the enemy. It is a plan against us.

Many of our false burdens are in the area of finances. We are not to get in the way of God's dealing in someone's life. Sometimes we pay for things that are not our responsibility. This could enable someone to continue in their bad habits or prevent them from getting desperate enough to seek God's provision for themselves. By spending our money on false burdens we could be sacrificing our blessings and we haven't saved for a vacation or a purchase we need to make.

We go places and do things that God is not asking us to do because of the false burden and responsibility. Many times fear is the root cause; but, as we become more secure in our relationship with the Lord, we become free to do only what the Lord requires of us.

The Lord let me know I had interfered in His dealing with people that I felt responsible for. "But, but – somebody has to do something!" I didn't know that we could turn people over to the Lord completely and let Him deal with them. I felt it was my responsibility to prevent them from making mistakes.

Maybe since we had a role as a parent in instructing our children when they were young it has led to us taking on false responsibility. "Don't touch that – it's hot!"; "It's nap time, you are tired."; "Don't waste your money on that cheap toy, it will break in two days!" Now, we are still trying to do it with adults – our grown children for example. There comes a time that we cut them loose and say, "You do it, Holy Spirit!" He is able to deal with us and convict us of sin and we must trust Him to lead and direct others. If they disappoint us again, it is up to the Lord to deal with them, and He will.

One evening as I was pruning and pulling off the dead parts from my plants, it was like a prophetic picture of me pulling things off my life that I had taken on or were only meant for a season. So I prayed specifically about what came to my mind.

If we ask Him, the Holy Spirit will remind us to let things go. Jesus is the burden bearer. That means His people are not to pick up each other's burdens. It admonishes us in 1 Peter 5:7b (NKJ): *casting all your care upon Him, for He cares for you.* Jesus said in Matthew 11:30 (NKJ): *My yoke is easy and My burden is light.*

There is a legitimate responsibility and there is an illegitimate one. One requires response. One is dead weight.

Prayer: *I cast the whole of my care (all my anxieties, all my worries, all my concerns, once and for) all on the Lord, for He cares for me affectionately and cares about me watchfully.* (Based on 1 Peter 5:7 AMP)

"I lay down my reputation and the desire to be respected and liked by everyone."

"I lay down my concern as to whether others are happy with everything I do."

"I lay down the need to be understood."

"I have done things to try to prevent rejection, and I don't want to do that anymore."

"Lord, help me to let it all go. I repent for not giving things to

You and worrying about them instead." (Name the things that come to your mind.)

Declare: I refuse to take on *false* responsibility for anyone and anything. I cut myself loose from the strings from the past, the fact that someone is family, or thinking *someone* needs to do it. I cut myself loose from fear of rejection, fear of retaliation or repercussions, in Jesus name. I am secure in You. You will never leave me nor forsake me. I am thoroughly loved and accepted by You, and I leave the rest of mankind in Your hands. Everyone is responsible for their own responses and reactions to the truth and even to react and respond correctly to someone else's behavior. It is not my responsibility to tiptoe around them and be careful not to offend them. Set me free, Lord, to follow after You and not these false burdens and responsibilities. Amen.

What Are You Responsible For?

If we give up false responsibilities, then we have the grace to take up what is our legitimate responsibility. When we carry false responsibilities there is not enough energy, time, or money to do what we really are gifted or called to do. Many times we have something we are asked to do, and then we add to it. Here is an exercise that will help to clarify things for you.

Take a sheet of paper and answer these questions or type it out. Give it some thought and take your time.

What is your responsibility? When I did this I broke it down into sections such as follows:

- My home: (listed my responsibilities, i.e., provide meals, maintain the house, keep up the laundry, water the plants, etc.)

- My job: tax reports, manage the office, do proposals as needed, etc.

- My church: (list what you have volunteered to do or where you serve and exactly what that responsibility entails.)

- Any other groups you serve in – if you are a leader, what is the job description (particular things you are responsible to do)?

- If you have children at home, you have responsibilities as a parent to train and teach them right from wrong, how to groom themselves, how to behave and other things.

- When your children are grown, things shift and as adults they are responsible for their own food, shelter, clothing, and provision. Some of you may have to pray this through to a reality.

Type up exactly what you are responsible to do and print it out.

If we clarify what we are responsible to do, we won't step in and take up someone else's duties. This takes discipline. I noticed when I finished with my list, there were no people on there that I was responsible for. I'm not responsible for anyone else's behavior, their actions, or their problems. I'm not responsible to change anyone and while I am accountable for the things on my list, I am not accountable for anything *not* on the list.

Another Angle on False Responsibility

There is another "care" that we need to cast on the Lord. We cannot change ourselves. We can ask God to change us and cooperate with Him but we must let Him do the work. Lord, You expect us to surrender and give You our best. You will do the rest.

Having begun in the Spirit, are you now being made perfect by the flesh? (Galatians 3:3 NKJ)

He who has begun a good work in you will complete it until the day of Jesus Christ (Philippians 1:6 NKJ)

Prayer: I am powerless to change myself, but I am in covenant with You. In this covenant, I am the weak, small one. You are the One who will help me. It is me that You want. All of me, completely yielded. I confess that I have been double-minded. I renounce all religion and religious duty and every counterfeit to a living relationship with You.

Chapter 9

Rejection

My Story

A few years ago, while having a conversation with a Christian leader whom I greatly respected, I said, "The Lord has shown me that you and I will minister together." At that moment a contemplative look came over her face and she began to ponder the thought. Suddenly, I was flooded with feelings that came out of nowhere! I wished that my words had never been uttered. I wanted to run and was fighting back tears. I got away from there as quickly as I could.

As I made my way to my car in the parking lot, I cried out to the Lord and asked what in the world that was about. It was then that a memory came back to me of myself at age twelve. There was a guy named Jeffrey that liked me and wanted to "go steady." That was fine with me because it was the popular thing to do, and I wore his ring on a chain hanging around my neck. One day, he decided that he wanted to kiss me, and that was too much! I broke up with him.

A year later, he was "going steady" with someone else. She looked a lot more mature than I did. I have had the gift of looking younger than my age. However, I didn't see it as a gift at age twelve! Already knowing the answer to my question, I walked up to the girl and asked if she was going steady with Jeffery and she said, "Yes." I said, "I used to go with him." She threw her head back and in a mocking tone said, "*You?*" That was a horrible feeling to be addressed with such unbelief and disdain. And there I was thirty-five years later having a flashback of emotion. With just the look of pondering on this present day woman's face, I felt as if she was going to say the same thing as that girl did thirty-five years ago!... "*You?*"

Riding home in my car that night, I forgave the girl who had hurt my feelings so many years ago, and asked the Lord to heal me. I have found that using the incidents and pain of the present have helped me deal with the past.

The root cause of some of my problems was rejection. Like many other people I experienced rejection before birth. I was the third child born to my parents in three years. My mother was *not* happy to find out she was pregnant with me. Although she took good care of me, I grew up thinking that God must have made a mistake and put me in the wrong family. I did not feel like I was loved and wanted.

When we suffer with rejection, every event and circumstance is filtered through that mindset. The word "reject" according to Webster means "to throw back." Rejection produced a fear in me that whatever I did would not be received and accepted, but instead it would be thrown back. This led me to be a people-pleaser and to strive for perfection. Seeking perfection became as crippling as the fear of rejection. Because I was afraid of not getting it perfect, I would procrastinate. Also any words of correction or criticism made me feel rejected.

CHOICE: To overcome rejection, we have to renew our minds with the truth of the Word of God. Here is an example of how to do it. While people may reject us, our God never will.

Praise be to God, Who has not rejected my prayer or withheld His love from me! (Psalm 66:20 NIV)

For the Lord will not reject His people; He will never forsake His inheritance. (Psalm 94:14 NIV)

Though my father and mother forsake me, the Lord will receive me. (Psalm 27:10 NIV)

These verses tell us the truth. We must respond to the truth. If you have a problem with rejection, talk this through with the Lord and ask Him to heal you. Then memorize Scripture that replaces the wrong thinking. You can personalize these verses in the following way:

"The Lord will not reject me because I belong to Him. He will never forsake His inheritance!" and *"Praise be to God, who has not rejected my prayer or withheld His love from me! Though others forsake me, the Lord will receive me."*

Rejection Protection

My Story

Weeping over greeting cards! How sappy is that? There I sat with my collection of treasures in our beach rental. These cards were from previous Mother's Days, wedding anniversaries, and birthdays. I only saved the ones perceived to be sincere and heartfelt at the time I received them. Not that I *believed* what people had written in them. I certainly did not feel all that lovable. They were just being sweet, I thought. But, something had happened to me. I sat there reading them, *knowing* that I was loved and appreciated, and my heart was so touched.

I had built walls to protect myself from pain, but they had kept love out, too. "Rejection protection" devices have been detrimental. Instead of coming to our Creator and being honest with Him and believing He could heal us, many of us took the enemy's suggestion to protect ourselves from any further hurt. This habit pattern continues from then onward. More and more protection devices get put into place until we can no longer be tormented with what someone else does. We refuse to care. Rejecting others is part of "protection." Some of us decide, "You can't reject me because I reject you first."

In the process of walling out the ones who could hurt us, we have kept out the good things that we could receive too – like the sincere expression of appreciation. We can't hear it because of the echoes of painful memories. We end up with a little cup with which to measure out and receive love. This limits the amount of joy we are capable of experiencing. Getting healed helps us do away with the "rejection protection" devices. The reason for this is that once we realize we can be healed no matter what happens, the fear diminishes.

Another one of our "rejection protection" devices is to isolate ourselves to keep from being hurt again. This works to a degree. The only problem is that we take the hurt into isolation with us. It doesn't go away and the fear of being hurt again serves as a confirmation that this is just the way it needs to be. Most of the time, this is unconscious behavior.

Unforgiveness may not be something a person is aware of. It is usually when the Lord points it out to us through a counselor or while we are in prayer, or maybe just riding down the road. Forgiving and asking God to heal us needs to be done at the same time so that healing will begin and a release experienced.

Holding unforgiveness against someone – even ourselves – is a form of punishment. Statements like "I will never forgive them for that," feel justified at the time and seem to help. But the principles of the Bible are being violated, and since that means we are cooperating with the enemy, we get into more trouble with this behavior. This opens the door in our life to other things to make our feelings stronger – such as hate or bitterness. This can go beyond just holding on to the offense. It can get to the place where we are retaliating by saying things to influence others to feel the way we do about another person. Or we do things to "get even." Thank God, we can be delivered from this!

Prayer: Help me deal with the things that hold me back, Lord. I want to be free.

Chapter 10

Breaking the Ties That Bind

What kind of things represent "ties that bind"? Generational curses, words spoken over us, soul-ties, and vows we have made. This is an interactive chapter and you and your family can be set free as you pray the prayers.

Generational Ties

In Exodus 34:6-7 (NKJ), it says that God revealed Himself to Moses. *And the Lord passed before him and proclaimed, "The Lord, the Lord God, merciful and gracious, longsuffering, and abounding in goodness and truth, keeping mercy for thousands, forgiving iniquity and transgression and sin, by no means clearing the guilty, **visiting the iniquity of the fathers upon the children and the children's children to the third and the fourth generation.**"*

This means that our ancestors have done things and we are reaping the consequences – good and bad – believe it or not!

Here is an example from my family tree:

My great-grandmother got a divorce for no reason that we were able to ascertain.

My grandmother was married five times.

My mother was married four times.

I got married three times.

I have four siblings and there are eleven marriages between them.

This all originated with a covenant being broken by my great-grandmother, and the generational curse was passed down.

- Just to let you know, I broke the curse over me and my descendants, and my husband and I have been married for 37 years!

Other people see financial problems and poverty running through their family. Some have serious illnesses. They call this hereditary, but there are spiritual dynamics at work. There are those who have been in secret societies and made vows and oaths, and their descendants suffer for it. Some families have sexual abuse and it keeps showing up again and again. Some people have occult influence. For instance, the occult, hypnotism, and astrology fascinated my grandmother. I didn't know about it until later in my life. But, when I was a girl growing up, I was drawn to books in the school library on witches and supernatural phenomenon. As an adult, before becoming a Christian, I went to fortune tellers.

- I repented and was set free and broke this curse of being drawn into the occult off of my family.

Words Spoken Over Us

In the book of James, we are told that the tongue has the power to bless or curse. How many negative things have you or other people spoken over your life? Some people, when they were children, had adults speak over them that they would never amount to anything. These negative words have power over us.

Some people even pray things out of the will of God and hinder us or God's work. Here is an example. Years ago, I attended a youth meeting at my Spirit-filled church. It was a talent show and many of the parents attended. The presence of the Lord came very strongly at one point, and an anointing came on me to give a message from the Lord. I wanted to be obedient but could not step out of my aisle. Something was holding me back and it wasn't me and it wasn't the Lord.

The Lord later told me that someone had prayed against anything like this happening. They were probably operating in fear that it might offend their parents or something, but there is power in words. Someone muttering over and over under his or her breath,

"God, don't let anyone prophesy. Don't let anyone prophesy," is actually hindering the Holy Spirit.

It also happened to me a few years later, that I would begin to speak to someone and share what the Lord was telling me and when I spoke, my words would be jumbled and confusing even to me – making me wish I had never even tried to share it.

Later on, I was in a meeting receiving prayer and the minister had something revealed to him from the Lord about me. It was this: "It is as if someone has placed a spell over you and prayed against you and called you a Jezebel. It is someone who is jealous of you and does not believe you, as a woman, should minister. I break this off you in Jesus name."

- I was set free from the power of these witchcraft prayers, prayed by an ignorant Christian.

I pray the following on a regular basis and suggest you do the same: "I break every word-curse that has been spoken over me, in Jesus name. I cancel every prayer that is not in accordance with the plan and purpose of God for my life."

Soul-Ties (A Link or Connection)

Soul-ties are formed when we give our heart or body to someone. Ideally, we give our heart and body to our spouse, and that is the only God-sanctioned soul-tie a woman should have with a man and vice-versa. God instituted sexual intercourse to seal the covenant of marriage. The Bible teaches that having sex is becoming one with that person.

Or do you not know that he who is joined to a harlot is one body with her? For "the two," He says, "shall become one flesh." 1 Corinthians 6:16 (NKJ)

When we have sex with someone we make a soul-tie with that person. As a result, there are people who are still "tied" to someone, and have had dreams about their ex-husband or ex-wife, or former lovers. The good news is that these soul-ties can be broken. If you want to be set free from any soul-ties, you can pray the following prayer.

Prayer: Father God, I repent for any sex I have participated in outside of the covenant of marriage. I sever all soul-ties and command any ungodly attachments to leave me in Jesus name. I sever the soul-tie to (name) in Jesus name and cut myself loose from any attachment.

As we have gone through life, we have given our heart to first this one and then another as relationships are made and broken. Sometimes we idolize a person (spiritual leader, Hollywood star, or even a friend). It is also possible to allow someone to control us or a part of our life. Perhaps there is a soul-tie that needs to be severed with someone else from your past. If you want to be set free from any other ungodly soul-ties, here is a prayer for you.

Prayer: Lord, I repent for idolizing or allowing (name) to control my life, and by an act of my will I cut myself loose from all ungodly soul-ties and influence. I command all strings attached to me to be severed in Jesus name.

Confession and Decree for Entire Family

This is a confession of repentance and it is only necessary to do it once.

Since repentance brings deliverance, I wrote out a confession and decree to pray over our entire extended family. Daniel did this for the nation of Israel and I modified his prayer in Daniel 9:1-16 (NIV) along with what God was looking for in Isaiah 58:6-14 (NIV). I began with confessing the sins that I knew that my family had done.

I confess the sins that my people and I have done against You. Oh God, we have done our own thing. We have put worthless things before our eyes. We have been conformed to this world and not to the image of Jesus Christ. We have been passive and complacent. We have wallowed in unbelief. We have held hands with the enemy as we spoke against others. We have forsaken the living waters and well of salvation and dug our own leaky cisterns. We have been self-centered and not cared about the lost and hurting world around us. We have fasted the things of the spirit and gorged ourselves on the things of this world. We have lied, cheated on income tax, criticized people, judged, been foolish with money, been concerned with what others think more than what *You* think. We have committed sexual sins. We have not been good stewards of the gifts you gave us. We have been bored with You and fascinated with the entertainment of this world.

So I turn to You, Lord God and plead with You in prayer and petition, in fasting, and in humility. I pray to You, my God and confess: O Lord, the great and awesome God, who keeps His covenant of love with all who love Him and obey His commands, we have sinned and done wrong. We have been wicked and have rebelled; we have turned away from Your commands and laws. We have not listened to Your servants the prophets, who spoke in Your name to our kings, our princes and our fathers, and to all the people of the land.

Lord, You are righteous, but this day we are covered with shame. We have been scattered because of our unfaithfulness to You. O Lord, we as Your people are covered with shame because we have sinned against You. You, Lord, our God are merciful and forgiving, even though we have rebelled against You; we have not obeyed the Lord our God or kept the laws He gave us through His servants the prophets. All of us have transgressed Your law and turned away, refusing to obey You. Therefore the curses and sworn judgments written in the Law of Moses, the servant of God, have been poured out on us, because we have sinned against You.

You have fulfilled the words spoken against us and against our rulers by bringing upon us great disaster. Just as it is written in the Law of Moses, all this disaster has come upon us, yet we have not sought the favor of the Lord our God by turning from our sins and giving attention to Your truth. You did not hesitate to bring the disaster upon us, for You, Lord our God, are righteous in everything You do, yet we have not obeyed You.

Now, O Lord our God, who brought Your people out of Egypt with a mighty hand and then sent Jesus to pay for our sins and the result of them, we have sinned, we have done wrong.

O Lord, in keeping with all Your righteous acts, turn away Your anger and Your wrath from this family. Our sins and the iniquities of our fathers have made us an object of scorn to all those around us in the spirit world.

Now, our God, hear the prayers and petitions of Your servant. For Your sake, O Lord, look with favor on Your desolate sanctuary. Give ear, O God, and hear; open Your eyes and see the desolation in our lives. We are people who bear Your name. We do not make requests of You because we are righteous in ourselves, but because of Your great mercy and what Jesus has done. O Lord, listen! O Lord, forgive! O Lord, hear and act! For Your sake, O my God, do not delay, because we as a people bear Your Name.

Decree

*This decree can be used periodically to speak
righteousness over your entire family.*

I decree that we will be a people who will loose the chains of injustice and untie the cords of the yoke, to set the oppressed free and break every yoke. We will share our food with the hungry and provide the poor wanderer with shelter – when we see the naked, we will clothe him, and will not turn away from our own flesh and blood. Then our light will break forth like the dawn, and our healing will quickly appear; then our righteousness will go before us, and the glory of the Lord will be our rear guard. Then we will call, and the Lord will answer us. We will cry for help, and He will say, "Here am I."

We will do away with the yoke of oppression, with the pointing finger and malicious talk, and we will spend ourselves in behalf of the hungry and satisfy the needs of the oppressed, then our light will rise in the darkness, and our night will become like the noonday. The Lord will guide us always; He will satisfy our needs in a sun-scorched land and will strengthen our frame.

We will be like a well-watered garden, like a spring whose waters never fail. Our people will rebuild the ancient ruins and will raise up the age-old foundations; we will be called Repairer of Broken Walls, Restorer of Streets with Dwellings. We will call entering the Lord's Sabbath rest a delight and the Lord's holy ways honorable, and we will honor Him by not going our own way and not doing as we please or speaking idle words, then we will find our joy in the Lord, and You will cause us to ride on the heights of the land and to feast on our inheritance in Jesus Christ.

Chapter 11

Brokenness and Humility – The Road to Ministry

*I*n individual ministry, the more we grow and expand the more often we need to spend time with the Lord. We must increase what we do for strength and to feed our spirit. There will be a temptation to fear, or to want to go back to safety. We must be courageous for God is with us.

There are different stages that God takes us through to make us ready for ministry. Misunderstanding, being overlooked, and failure produce brokenness and humility. These are qualities that are precious to God.

My Story

Over the years, in my quiet times with the Lord, He spoke to me through Scriptures and to my heart that He had a tremendous call on my life. When I would go a Christian meeting somewhere else, a speaker with a prophetic anointing would call me out of a crowd of strangers. He or she would say something to the effect, "God has a call on your life, and He is sending you to the nations." I wanted so badly for my own pastor to recognize my gifts and calling. I was looking for approval from a person. When we do this, God will see to it that the person cannot see the gift in you. It is also humbling.

In my home church, it was taught that women were not God's first choice in ministry and that we were pretty much limited to teaching other women and children. I continued wanting the approval and recognition, and I couldn't get it. The leader became very critical of me and so I decided to leave my church. I resigned from the leadership position I had, turned in my key to the church, and gave up all that I was involved in. I was also tired of the misunderstanding about my prophetic gifting.

Note:

This is nothing against the pastor who was in place at the time. Perhaps God wanted to put His hand over a person's eyes so that he could not recognize what He had put in me or called me to do. God's plan for my life was not always easy. God wanted to break something in me – I wanted and needed a person's approval.

It seems we get on a path with God and decide we don't like the path we are on because it is painful and decide to get on our own path. Take it from me, if you want to know what painful really is – get off the God-ordained path! If you want to find out what the back side of the desert is like, just wander on out there!

So I left my church and began again at a new one. I was very involved, promoted, and even was interviewed from time to time along with others during a morning service and was asked, "Why do you attend this church, and why have you stayed so long?" I would say, "As a woman I am free to minister at this church." It was all about ministry. It was not about the perfect will of God, it was about a door open for me. I got away from God's plan because I didn't want to suffer. After five and a half years, there was a prophetic conference and those who were registered were to receive prophetic ministry beforehand. God had been trying to talk to me, but you know how we are – selective hearing – especially if it is a husband the Lord is trying to talk to us through! It can't be God – what do they know? (Smile.) In the midst of this, my husband had already started visiting back at the church we had left five and half years previous.

Now back to the prophetic ministry I received... The man said to me, among other things, "You have traded intimacy *with* God for ministry *for* God. You traded your walk with God for an open door in ministry." I felt like a sword went into me – a two-edged sword. God's was trying to kill and to heal something in me at the same time. I had been burning the candle at both ends to serve the Lord.

At one point my husband had "graded" me – which really made me mad! He had taken a sheet of paper and listed my gifts and graded how well I was using them. I didn't get good grades! I was on my way to church that day after being "graded." I said "God, what he said is true, but I am mad!" And it was because he said to me, "You cannot see the forest for the trees!" I had put church in front of my family. I could not even pray about whether I was to be at a meeting, because I was in leadership and was required to be in that meeting. I couldn't even ask God! I had put these leaders on a pedestal. After the prophetic word, I cried for two days. I wrote a letter to the pastors. In the letter I told them what God had been dealing with me about and that my husband felt like it was time for us to leave the church, and that we were returning to our former church. (If you ever leave a church, you need to leave "right" by explaining to the pastor(s) – don't just disappear.)

This was an extremely painful time for me and when I returned to my former church, I knew that I was not to look for something to *do*. I had been doing and doing and doing, and now I needed to *be*. All this produced brokenness in me. A quality that is precious to God.

Control

My Story

A number of years ago through prophetic ministry, it was revealed to me by the Lord that I had a problem with *control* in my life. He said there were things that I had been praying about for years, with no apparent answer coming forth. The reason was that I was praying but not releasing the Lord to do what He knew was best. The Lord then said, "There are things you want to happen so bad, you even try to *make* them happen." He went on to say that this sealed my prayers in a concrete-like state and until I decided I would trust the Lord and release things to Him, these answers were going to continue to be suppressed.

This certainly got my attention and after getting over my initial reaction which was comprised of fear and anger, I began the process of overcoming this obstacle in my walk with the Lord. God had indicated that He would take me down a road to challenge me to see if I would really trust Him. This caused fear to rise up in me as to what the future would hold. The anger resulted from the Lord bringing this prophetic word about control in front of my husband. Normally the Lord corrected me privately. My pride did not like that!

What the Lord had in mind in delivering me from control was much more than what I expected. He wanted to deliver me from fear and bring me to a place of rest. He wanted me to *cease striving and know that He is God.* I discovered that there would be no *rest* unless I trusted Him. Trusting Him was impossible if there was doubt about His intention and love. And so, the process began of Him patiently showing me His love in spite of my failures and weaknesses. I found that I could trust Him.

I prayed that the Lord would bring the situations in my life to turn me back to Him and away from controlling my life and circumstances. I acknowledged being powerless to change myself. I was still afraid, but decided to be courageous, in spite of it. *"God gives grace to the humble,"* I reminded myself. And grace was certainly what I needed!

I heard about a book by Lisa Bevere: *Out of Control and Loving It.* I never read the book but I was driving down the road one day and the title came to me and I said to the Lord, "I'm out of control and I *hate* it! I do not like being out of control."

Hebrews 10:31 (NKJ) says, *It is a fearful thing to fall into the hands of the living God.* Do you know why? He is in control – not you! It is fearful if we are a control freak, but if we want to trust Him and rest, it is a wonderful thing after we learn to surrender things to Him.

I found out that my attempts to "keep peace" between my husband and his parents were another area of control. I did everything I could to keep conflict at a minimum and to prevent tempers from flaring. When I let go – sure enough things exploded, but they got over it.

At another point in my Christian journey, the Lord told me I was "riding the brakes." He said He wanted to take my life forward at a greater speed, but this was hindering me. Then He said, "Not only that, but when I want to steer your life in a different direction, you grab the steering wheel. And when I start to turn, you hold the wheel straight ahead."

I said, "Oops. I guess I thought You wouldn't notice."

Giving up control was difficult. At another stage in my Christian growth, the Lord told me I was afraid. Having dealt with much fear in my life, I wasn't surprised by His statement but wasn't aware of an area. He said, "You are afraid you will lose control of your life." He said, "You *don't have* control of your life, so this is an irrational fear. You can't lose something you don't have!"

Prayer: Lord, I want to surrender my life fully to You, and do not want to hinder my prayers by operating in "control."

Ignorance, Apathy & Unbelief

I discovered some of the tactics of the enemy against Christians. These three things can greatly interfere with our development and growth as followers of the Lord.

- *Ignorance* means you don't know.

- *Apathy* means you don't care.

- *Unbelief* means you don't believe.

A Story

What if you had a rich relative in Pensacola, Florida? You were their only living relative and rather than let the State get all their money, they left it to you. They died and it was determined that you were the sole heir. But the person who was supposed to tell you was not able to convince you of the truth. You never even heard of the relative before so you ignored the letter that came. You lived your life in poverty. You barely were able to make ends meet. You had an old car that you had to pray for to keep it running. You saw people in need but couldn't do anything to help them. You were forced to steal food a couple of times just to survive.

Ignoring the good news made you oblivious to how things really were. Finally, one day you decided, "Hey, what do I have to lose?" And sure enough the inheritance was yours! You had lost a few teeth because you couldn't afford to go to the dentist. You had hurt your back doing a job only a donkey should do and your life is almost over. It didn't have to be that way.

Ignorance can be cured by becoming aware of the truth. Jesus provided so much more than salvation from hell. He has provided for us victory: for our body, soul, and spirit. Ignorance of what He has provided has cost us dearly.

My people are destroyed for lack of knowledge (Hosea 4:6a NKJ).

Through the redemption of the cross, Jesus completely defeated satan. Our victory over all the plans of the enemy has been accomplished. We have the power of the Holy Spirit to enable us to live a victorious Christian life. However, when I looked at my life, there was something wrong with the picture. What happened? I found out that ignorance was not a good thing!

Experientially, we have the opportunity to "get in on" what Jesus paid for. Let me explain. We are in a struggle. *For we do not wrestle against flesh and blood, but against principalities, against powers, against the rulers of the darkness of this age, against spiritual hosts of wickedness in the heavenly places.* (Ephesians 6:12

NKJ) So we grow, we learn, we appropriate the things the Lord has already accomplished, and we overcome!

My Story

- Jesus died on the cross for my sins. I had to be convicted of sin and convinced by the Holy Spirit that I needed a Savior in order to be saved. I prayed to accept the Lord in April 1974. But when was salvation provided for by Jesus? It was over 2,000 years ago.

- I first received a miraculous healing in 1977. When did Jesus accomplish the work? It took place when He took the stripes on His back. 1 Peter 2:24 (NKJ) says *who Himself bore our sins in His own body on the tree, that we, having died to sins, might live for righteousness – by whose stripes you were healed.*

- I was baptized in the Holy Spirit in 1977, after being a Christian for three years. It was a gift that I had to receive. However, it has been available since the Day of Pentecost.

- The yoke of the enemy was destroyed over me, but in my ignorance I continued to walk in bondage because I did not know any better.

Apathy causes us to do nothing about our situation. This lack of concern makes us spiritually lazy. Lethargy is a spirit that has been assigned to us spiritually. It is a state of dullness. We lack spiritual energy, activity, or enthusiasm.

Unbelief causes us to pare down our vision and hope for the future. It causes us to doubt what God has spoken to us and whether it will ever come to pass. This is an outright attack against our faith.

We must not accept these things as the mindset of a normal Christian life. These are spirits sent to rob us of our destiny. Half the battle is realizing what we are dealing with and how it affects us. The other half is conquering it.

Prayer: I do not want to be ignorant of all that God has provided for me. I pray for a teachable spirit. I break all agreement with lethargy and complacency, and renounce these spirits. I refuse to walk in unbelief! It is partnership with the demonic! Joy is my faith gauge. I have joy in believing! I command all unbelief to leave me in Jesus name. I will not cast away my confidence, for it has great reward! I choose to believe regardless of what I see.

SECTION TWO:
BETWEEN YOU AND GOD

Chapter 12

God Enjoys Relationship

The Lord would like to have an intimate relationship with each of us. Just so you know what I am talking about, I looked up the meaning of the word, "intimate." It denotes closeness and friendship. Synonyms for intimacy are affection, affinity, communion, confidentiality, understanding, companionship, fellowship, and togetherness. Doesn't that sound good?

My Story

At the time this event took place I had been a Christian for 22 years and had experienced times of walking close to the Lord. It had been a very busy season of my life, and I thought that my "busyness" was why I felt distant from Him. It was like we had a deal, "I do my part, and Lord, You do Your part." I really wanted more in our relationship.

I set aside time to be alone with the Lord, fasted breakfast, took off from work and sat down for what I expected to be a great time with Him – just like in the old days! However, when I got quiet it felt superficial. As time went by, I began to get agitated and felt like a complainer. Then slowly drowsiness, cynicism and boredom surrounded me. The Lord suggested that I prepare myself a cup of tea so that I would be more alert.

I started thinking about intimacy. My definition was being able to share "heart to heart."

I looked over some notes I had written. "What destroys intimacy?" Then the answer: "Broken trust." When someone betrays our trust, it results in the holding back of our true thoughts and feelings.

I thought about broken trust with a leader over me in church and how I was unable to get involved and trust leaders in ministry again. I thought of friends who had broken my trust in them. Then I realized I felt like God had not honored my trust in Him. At that moment, a question popped into my head as the Lord asked, "What about Me? Have I broken your trust?" I immediately reacted with "We don't want to go there!" It was then that I became aware of my feelings toward the Lord. I felt like God had not honored my trust in Him. My mind began to explode with thoughts. The Lord gently said, *"Tell Me."* I was struggling at this point and could not suppress it any longer. I blurted out, "Back at my previous church, I did everything You told me to do. I trusted You for a breakthrough in that church!" I continued to struggle with this because I knew and respected God and was trying to be careful with how I was saying things and yet He was prodding me to be honest. Gently He responded, "What else?"

"I trusted You to heal Emily (my 40 year-old friend who died of cancer) and Charlie (my mother's husband). I also believed concerning other things that if I did what You told me to, it would be worth it and that ultimately You would vindicate me openly!"

Whoa! Where did that come from? I didn't intend to say all that, or to be tearfully emotional as I did it. I was surprised as the Lord gently asked, "What else?"

"I've wasted my life. My family has thought I was a fool. Where is the fruit I was promised? Where is the power? I went everywhere I could go – to every conference and meeting. I did everything I could do. I've been out there on the front line – alone. Not feeling that any other human understood me. You are all-powerful, all-knowing, and You could have helped me…"

Again, His tender response was, "What else?" This went on for a while as I emptied my barrel of unresolved issues. Part of the time I was apologizing to the Lord for having all this against Him. Then He would ask me again, "What else?" Eventually I got to the bottom of it all and my barrel was empty.

Later, I recorded all this in my journal and continued my conversation with the Lord. "Whew! I didn't know all that was in me! How disgusting. I'm sorry that I felt this way, Lord. Finally I am honest about it."

"Oh, Lord…there's more – I trusted You to heal my eyes, allergies, and to do other things. You could have prevented me from being deceived. I made a fool of myself! I was a total failure in areas of ministry. You could have prevented things from happening in my family like they did. Now I don't trust anybody!"

What Had Happened to Me?

I grew up wounded from childhood. Looking back as an adult, the incidents seem so trivial, but the hurt and pain were real. The same goes with my walk with God. I was hurt in my spiritual "childhood," misunderstanding my Father and His plans. I was hurt by some of His children – some of it was real, some imagined. But the pain was there just the same. It hindered my relationship with people, with God, and with His church. So just like I needed healing from my natural childhood, I needed healing from my spiritual childhood.

I had to forgive myself for my part in all the failure. And I forgave God for all the things I had held against Him. I asked Him to heal my hurts and disappointments, and He spoke to me about why He had permitted suffering in my life. I believe it all came down to this: I needed a compassionate heart. And He said to me, "I have seen your suffering and I cried with you. I have felt your pain, but I have known what was best." He promised me that much fruit would come forth from my life as a result of the suffering. The words that the Lord spoke to me brought healing and began the restoration of our relationship.

I started to heal, and over a period of time was restored to Him being my first love. Later on I asked the Lord, "What would hinder someone the most in their walk with You?"

His response was: "To get offended with Me, be distracted from intimacy with Me, and get disappointed with prayer." All three of these things had succeeded against me. It took being honest with God to get back to where I needed to be. He is so wonderful and merciful and restored the joy of my salvation!

It is impossible to live in this day and time and not be injured in some way while serving the Lord. Disillusionment can be the result of disappointment with people and God! Depending on the call on your life, I would venture to say that dealing with these kinds of issues could just be part of your preparation for ministry. So, no matter what state you find yourself in, there is hope! God says in Jeremiah 29:11 (NIV 1984), *"For I know the plans I have for you," declares the LORD, "plans to prosper you and not to harm you, plans to give you hope and a future."*

The enemy has access into our lives through the wounds we experience. These wounds can be the result of the death of someone or the way we have been treated or mistreated, and the result of life's circumstances. If we forgive and ask the Lord to heal us, the enemy loses his power. If we become bitter and unforgiving, our wounds fester and the enemy torments us with pain. Not dealing with these things also hinders our love.

The Power of Choice

Many people are out of touch with issues that need to be dealt with, just like I was. We must choose to take the time to get alone with the Lord to be honest with Him about how we feel. He knows it already. We won't shock Him! We can tell Him if we are disappointed or feel that He let us down. We then choose to forgive Him.

He desires a close relationship with us and wants to heal us. He enjoys our presence so much. He enjoys our attention. He is blessed by our reaching out to Him in faith. He enjoys each individual's way of expressing him/herself in their own unique way. He enjoys *you*.

Prayer: Lord, You want a close relationship with me and want to heal and restore me. You enjoy spending time with me. You are happy when I reach out to You in faith. You enjoy how I express myself in my own unique way. You enjoy *me*! Help me to draw near to You with freedom to share my heart and to have You share Your heart with me.

Chapter 13

Intimacy with God

The secret place is where you find your *alone* time with the Lord. At first it is by faith that it is even real. But He assured me one day, "If you will give me *your* undivided attention, I will give you *My* undivided attention." After years of taking this time with the Lord, I found that my encouragement comes from there in His presence! My comfort, motivation, strength, sanity, life, and my joy come from Him.

We have heard of many Christian leaders falling in immorality. I wondered how someone greatly used by the Lord could get into deep sin. The Lord told me the safety against sin is the secret place. He wants us to meet with Him. This place with God is hidden from the enemy. It is there by being honest with Him when we have temptations, we can confess them and receive help in time of need. The enemy has kept people who are tempted out of God's presence with shame over the thoughts. Being ignorant of the schemes of the devil, they fall for his trick.

Another thing is that pride blinds God's people so that they cannot see what is happening. It is so obvious if you have "eyes to see." You will even laugh at the temptation because it is so obvious. And you knew better than to entertain the thoughts that would lead to sin.

Drawing Near

Now is the time! When we say we want more in our walk with God, we need to press in at that moment. We are not to treat it like it is a dream of something we want *one* day. There is no time like the present! When we say, "I love You" to God, we can demonstrate that love. We can be creative in how we do it. Religion wants us only to be satisfied with merely saying words. Jesus taught that if we loved Him we would obey Him. Love therefore can be demonstrated. And even when we mess up, we shouldn't shrink back from God's presence. He enjoys relationship. Our performance has never been a requirement for intimacy with God. He is not jealous or offended when we have other things to do. He is jealous when we go to something else for comfort and affirmation.

A Vision from the Lord

In my prayer time I had a vision that took place in heaven. A group of people walked up to me that had lived their life on earth and were now there. They had advice for me.

The first one said, "If you knew how valuable time was, you would not waste it."

Another said, "If you knew the power of love, you would love more."

The next one said, "Don't be afraid to jump, He will catch you."

Still another voice said to me, "Love like there is no tomorrow. These are lessons we learned too late. Please hear us! Time is short!"

Finding a Closer Relationship with God

So many of us don't even know that a closer walk with God is attainable. That relationship would not be the result of living a more holy life, but would come from taking down the walls that we have erected to keep a safe distance from Him. Why would these walls be built? Either out of fear of God (an unholy fear, not reverence), disappointment with God, feeling like God betrayed our trust in Him or His Word, or not knowing Him as He is. By sharing my journey with you, I hope to be able to unravel the web the enemy has created in making a close relationship with the Lord seem unattainable or too difficult to accomplish. We must remember it is the Lord who took the initiative to start a relationship with us.

> *For God so loved the world that He gave His only begotten Son* (John 3:16a NKJ)

> *No one can come to Me unless the Father who sent Me draws him* (John 6:44a NKJ)

> *While we were still sinners, Christ died for us.* (Romans 5:8b NKJ)

Many wrong thoughts have been planted in our minds by the enemy and those have caused us to believe inaccurate things about the Lord. I am writing this to those who have had a born-again experience with God, trusting in the crucifixion of Jesus to pay for sins and believing that on the third day He rose from the dead! So I am writing to believers.

That is a very important word: "believers." Our whole walk with God and what I am sharing with you is based on believing. We have believed that there are certain things we must do to please God. We must pray, fast, read our Bible, and go to church. Those things are for our own benefit! Praying will change things! Reading and studying the Bible will help us get to know the Lord and to understand His ways and increase our faith. Fasting will cause us to be more sensitive to the Spirit and help us to overcome our flesh, and cause breakthroughs to take place! But the Bible says that without faith it is impossible to please God. It didn't say without fasting it is impossible to please God, or without going to church it is impossible to please God.

But without faith it is impossible to please Him, for he who comes to God must believe that He is, and that He is a rewarder of those who diligently seek Him. (Hebrews 11:6b NKJ)

Being in relationship with the Lord is a living experience!

Father God

How We Relate to Our Earthly Father Is How We Relate to Our
Heavenly Father

My Story

When I was little, I enjoyed my daddy. He liked to build things for us kids. Once he constructed a stagecoach for us to ride in. He took us treasure hunting and we found arrowheads and relics from the Civil War. He was very creative and drew pictures to entertain us and we kids recorded "episodes" of *Gunsmoke* together on his reel to reel tape player with him. After we grew up, he didn't relate very well. Our relationship was awkward. He had divorced my mother and maybe this contributed to things. He seemed distant, stoic, and reserved. He never called or contacted me. However I made the effort to stay in touch so I called and sometimes drove the six hours to his city to visit him. He seemed happy to see me but these visits and phone calls were not satisfying. He was an introvert and had difficulty communicating and showing emotion. His hugs were about as responsive as hugging a tree.

Little did I know this influenced how I viewed my heavenly Father. I knew God liked me okay. I knew I could get in touch with Him and talk to Him in prayer, but felt He wasn't all that concerned about me. I had to change my mind in the way I viewed God.

150

The Bible says, "God is love." So He is what is described in 1 Corinthians 13:4-7 where we can read what love is. Choose to believe it is a description of His traits. "*God* is patient, *God* is kind..."

Jesus said, *He who has seen Me has seen the Father* (John 14:9 KJV). In this statement He is saying that their character and nature are the same. Jesus was approachable, caring and compassionate. He hated religion. He only got upset with his disciples because of their unbelief.

My opinion of God and how He views me is radically different now. I can say, I found my heavenly Father to be the kindest, most patient person I have ever met.

Religion vs. Relationship

Religion used to be a good word in my mind. When I was growing up, a person who was described as a religious person was one who loved God. But I see what religion has done to people and the term means something different to me now. It now reminds me of the mind-set that the Pharisees and Sadducees had in Jesus day. Religion can keep us from recognizing Jesus and prevent us from understanding what He is doing! Religion is a form of godliness that denies the power to have a relationship, power to change, power to walk with God, and power to overcome adversity.

So here we are in the present day, and religion is very strong. How does it influence us as Christians? Following are some ways we can identify its influence. We can become ensnared with legalism.

Obedience vs. Legalism

Obedience is hearing and obeying the Lord. Legalism is obeying rules – real or imagined, Biblical or self-made rules. *But man lives by every word that proceeds from the mouth of the* LORD. (Deuteronomy 8:3b and Matthew 4:4 NKJ)

We must *not* emphasize the letter of the law over the spirit of the law. Legalism is strict adherence to a literal interpretation of the law.

Religion causes us to do these things:

- We do all we know to please God and never feel like it is enough! That is a performance-based relationship. That is religion.
- We judge others and "grade" their spirituality. That is religion.
- We feel like we can approach God better if we have done the things on our checklist, such as praying, church attendance, and Bible reading. That is religion.
- We *don't* feel like we can approach God when we sense we haven't been "good." That is religion.
- We see things that we don't personally like in church and just *know* God doesn't like them either. That is religion.

The Lord said to me one day, "You have been diverted and caused to look away from the source of your help to again look at guilt and condemnation as a possible motivator! This is a religious spirit. Religion has never helped you fulfill My will and will *never* do it."

The most important thing is *sincere and pure devotion to Christ*. There is a battle to have this relationship. Since this is where our help comes from, the enemy strategically opposes us in this area.

Prayer: I take authority over all legalism. It will no longer govern me! It will not rule, preside over me, manage me, reign over me and control, dominate, and regulate my decisions. Get out of my life in the name of Jesus!

Grace

Then He (Jesus) called His twelve disciples together and gave them power and authority over all demons, and to cure diseases. (Luke 9:1 NKJ)

They did not earn this privilege. They were not "good" enough to deserve it. It was grace bestowed on them by the Lord. This same grace is working in our lives. However, if they hadn't gone out where He sent them, they never would have seen it.

So they departed and went through the towns, preaching the gospel and healing everywhere. (Luke 9:6 NKJ)

In the relationship we have with the Lord we are not to try to earn His favor, we are to just receive it. In order to get beyond this point, we must become fully aware that there is a big difference between religion and a daily living relationship with God. Maybe you have thought that people who acted like they were close to God were exaggerating or maybe you judged them as being too religious. If you want a closer walk with God, take the time now to repent.

Pray: Lord, I recognize that I have had wrong thoughts about what it means to be closer to You. I have been religious. I have judged other believers. Lord, there are things that You may have been doing that I judged wrongly because I did not recognize that it was You. Father, my access to Your presence is because of the blood of Jesus, not anything I have done or can do! I renounce the religious spirit and ask You to continue to set me free from its influence.

My Story

During the time that I had broken my intimacy with God, I was still praying and doing my Christian duties and had my check lists: read my Bible, pray. Religious duty replaces the relationship.

In order to break out of this I wrote the following to be spoken aloud every day:

Declaration: I renounce religion. Lord, I will meet with You daily, on purpose, and there will be a convergence. You are coming to the meeting, and I am coming, and there is going to be an exchange. I will give You my burdens and cast my cares on You, and You are just going to love on me. And You may even share something that is on Your heart with me. There is going to be a transformation when I meet with You, and a transfer. It is not that I just say my prayers; there is something that really happens. I declare You are going to lead me and guide me.

Chapter 14

Why Is It So Hard to Sit Down and Have a Focused Time with the Lord?

*P*erfectionism may be a problem. We want our time to just be perfect. We want no mind-wandering and unfinished business calling us and causing interruption. But it is a battle to even get there so we keep putting it off. We need to check our e-mail, make that phone call, or "Hey!" The house is screaming, "What about me? Doesn't anybody care that I'm dusty and cluttered right at this very moment and need your attention?" We think we don't have enough time to devote right now so instead of taking the 15 minutes we do have, we put it off.

We may try to do and say the things that seem to be what would draw the Presence of the Lord. It feels "canned" not fresh. We don't *feel* spiritual.

Prayer: Lord, I am just going to be honest with You. I love You and I want to spend time with You. I want to give You my undivided attention right now. Holy Spirit, I ask for Your assistance. I am powerless and need You. I want to make the rest of my life to be so filled with You that it will be the restoration of the years the canker worm has eaten!

So I will restore to you the years that the swarming locust has eaten [...] (Joel 2:25 NKJ).

The Lord says:

- Seize the moment.
- Give Me your attention.
- Be honest with Me, but respectful.
- Humble yourself.
- Come in faith.
- Believe that you are welcome in My Presence.
- Believe that I am approachable.

We might as well be honest with Him. He knows about everyone, everywhere.

And there is no creature hidden from His sight, but all things are naked and open to the eyes of Him to whom we must give account. (Hebrews 4:13 NKJ)

Declare: I am free from keeping rules and regulations. It is a relationship that the Lord wants with me. He is approachable and we are welcome in His Presence.

But Jesus the Son of God is our great High Priest who has gone to heaven itself to help us; therefore let us never stop trusting Him. This High Priest of ours understands our weaknesses, since He had the same temptations we do, though He never once gave way to them and sinned. So let us come boldly to the very throne of God and stay there to receive His mercy and to find grace to help us in our times of need. (Hebrews 4:14-16 LB)

It takes grace to walk with God in a disciplined manner and spend time with Him on a regular basis.

God resists the proud, but gives grace to the humble. (James 4:6 NKJ)

• It takes faith.

But without faith it is impossible to please Him, for he who comes to God must believe that He is, and that He is a rewarder of those who diligently seek Him. (Hebrews 11:6 NKJ)

- He promises to meet you half way.

Draw near to God and He will draw near to you. (James 4:8a NKJ)

- Seize the moment.

For God says, Your cry came to Me at a favorable time, when the doors of welcome were wide open. I helped you on a day when salvation was being offered. Right now God is ready to welcome you. Today He is ready to save you. (2 Corinthians 6:2 LB)

How Do You Develop Intimacy with God?

To be honest, I have waited on a feeling at times to see if I was "connecting" with God, and when I didn't have a feeling, many times I did continue pressing in. Making lists daily helps me to get things accomplished and once I put God at the top of my list I became more consistent. I set aside time every morning to spend with God and kept my appointment because it was *our* time, not because of a feeling.

When I felt unworthy or shallow, I prayed "I plead the blood of Jesus over me. I'm here because of Your faithfulness. I'm here because You initiated this relationship. You sought me, drew me, and convicted me of my sins and need of forgiveness. You saved me! You want to talk to me and for me to talk to You. This is a wonderful relationship that You ordained for us to have! Now I am not waiting on a feeling. I'm here by faith. My faith pleases You."

To develop intimacy with the Lord, it takes faith. It takes time. The flesh doesn't really want to do this so it will rebel. The cost involved is fasting. This doesn't get God to do something. It makes us more sensitive spiritually because we are denying our flesh. It also helps us to see ourselves and to cooperate in honesty with the Lord.

Why Fast?

Fasting, prayer, and time with the Lord are absolutely necessary to maintain what we have and to advance beyond what we have.

There is a war between the flesh and the spirit. It is not the food that gives the flesh power, it is never saying "no" to the flesh that gives it power. Therefore taking authority over our flesh nature is very important.

For me fasting is not an option! I've looked up 1 Corinthians 9:27 in several versions of the Bible to describe why we must get the upper hand on our flesh nature. Even though my body doesn't want a hunger pain, to lose any sleep, or to suffer in any way and only wants special treatment, it is my slave and will submit!

I discipline my body and bring it into subjection (NKJ)

I buffet my body, and bring it into bondage (NASB)

I beat my body and make it my slave (NIV)

I keep under my body, and bring it in subjection (KJV)

I discipline my body like an athlete, training it to do what it should. Otherwise, I fear that after preaching to others I myself might be disqualified (NLT)

Many people start out well as Christians, but do not finish well. They never got the victory over their flesh.

Issues with God

We've Come Too Far to Turn Back, and Where Would We Go?

Many of us have experienced disaster, dealt with death, and other calamities. Some of us are disillusioned, our faith has been shaken, and we're disappointed because of delay.

My Story

I heard the Lord say to me one morning, "You have felt like I let you down when it comes to your family. Job felt the same way but he, like you, decided to trust and live on anyway."

I felt my emotions begin to churn within me. Feelings were rising up that I didn't know were there. I hadn't been able to identify what was hindering my relationship with the Lord. And with those statements, He had pinpointed the very thing that was wrong with me. I was on day twelve of the 21-Day "Fasting for Breakthrough."

I pulled myself together and said, "Lord, my life seems contrary to Your Word. Deuteronomy 28 says I would be blessed coming in and going out." (By now I was weeping.) "It says part of the blessing is that I will lend and not borrow, and would be the head and not the tail. That is *not* manifesting in my life. You said that healing was the children's bread, and I need healing. I've sown. I've fasted. I've prayed. I do admit, however, that I've wasted much of my life in passivity, complacency, and unbelief. But it seems everything moves slowly with *peace* being the only thing I have to show for all this."

I continued my response to what the Lord said. "I didn't know I felt this way, Lord. You are holy and right and if there is any failure it is on my part. Your ways are perfect and righteous. Heal my disappointment and clear the air between us. I forgive You for not doing things my way or as quickly as I wanted them done. All-powerful and all-knowing – You did not stop bad things from happening in my family, but I choose not to let this interfere in our relationship because I release You now from my judgment. Thank You for Your patience with me."

Tears came to my eyes during the day as I thought back over all this. Now I knew what had come between me and the Lord and it was true: I did feel God had let me down.

The next day I made this entry in my journal:

God said to me, "I stirred up something with you yesterday when I put My finger on what is between us. If you decide to go on *regardless,* you will go deeper and farther than you ever dreamed."

I felt the Lord's presence and responded to Him:

"I will meet You here in this place I have found myself. You have allowed what I would *not* have allowed. You have waited when I would *not* have waited. You have seemed to overlook what I would not have overlooked. You have delayed in what I would not have delayed. I recognize You as God. I release You from my judgment and forgive You for not doing things my way and on my schedule. You are God and I am not. My thoughts are lower and inferior to Your thoughts. My ways are lower and inferior to Your ways. Heal me of my disappointment..." and then words tumbled and I didn't know where they were coming from. "Heal me from my feelings of abandonment – it has felt that I'm left on my own."

I paused and then declared, "I will persevere in prayer! There is no shadow of turning with You. You are a covenant-keeping God and You are faithful!"

I wept for a few days thinking of my condition and finally prayed myself through this. I read God's response to Job's comments and realized once again that God doesn't owe me anything, and it humbled me. I felt better.

I read some more in the Book of Job. I said, "I cannot question You, Lord. You are Almighty God, and it all belongs to You. I gave myself to You and cannot question Your wisdom, Your delays, or Your purposes. I believe in You."

The next night I had a dream. I was driving a big, old sedan and I could hear my cell phone ringing. The problem is that it was in my purse in the trunk of the car. I was looking for a place to pull off to answer the call. I could not find a place and ended up going up a hill. The car slowed to a crawl so somehow I was using self-effort to try to reach the top of the hill. I had my foot all the way down on the gas and it didn't help. I reached out and was using either my hand or foot to attempt to push the car up the hill. I woke up.

Interpretation: The symbol of a vehicle we drive in a dream represents our life or ministry. The bottom line is that I was having a hard time answering the call on my life and self-effort was not helping. In my time with the Lord I began to feel comfort and love and acceptance. It took a while to relax. He is so patient with me.

"Will you trust Me? Will you let Me heal you and our relationship once again?"

"Oh yes, Lord. You are worth everything to me! Your presence is life! I need You desperately. I have lost my joy and motivation. Heal me! Restore to me the joy of my salvation – *You* are it!"

Chapter 15

Lifestyle Fasting

asting can help facilitate our cooperation with the Lord by enabling us to yield our will to His. We can then exercise self-control and govern our actions. For years I could so relate to Paul in Romans where he said, *I don't understand myself at all, for I really want to do what is right, but I can't.* (Romans 7:15 LB) It is obvious that he broke through and got the victory through Jesus Christ. I never heard anyone teach how he did it. It was always an excuse for us to rationalize our failings. How could I have the ability to break free from the power of the flesh, which was holding me back? The Scriptures teach that there is a very real struggle (war). The Bible contrasts the difference in the mind set on the flesh and the mind set on the Spirit.

For those who live according to the flesh set their minds on the things of the flesh, but those who live according to the Spirit, the things of the Spirit. For to be carnally minded is death, but to be spiritually minded is life and peace. Because the carnal mind is enmity against God; for it is not subject to the law of God, nor indeed can be. So then, those who are in the flesh cannot please God. (Romans 8:5-8 NKJ)

My best time with the Lord was early in the morning. I had known this for many years. I even had a prophet tell me once, "Your best time with the Lord is 5 A.M.!" Knowing that I had an appointment with the Lord at that time of day caused me years ago to attempt to get up to pray. I fell back to sleep in the most awkward positions as I tried to subdue my flesh! Sitting on the couch was a big mistake. "Zzzzzzzz." So, other times I attempted to sit at the desk. I awakened with my head on the books that were lying there. Then another time I got down on my knees to pray and fell asleep bent over with my head on the floor! I gave up and for years felt that one day I would have an appointment with the Lord early in the morning.

I needed to spend time alone with the Lord every day, but I could not discipline myself to do it. It seemed that busyness and a large family left me with no "set" time with God. At least that was my excuse. But we all know that we find time to do the things we want to do. This led to my discovery of the power of fasting. I also found out that fasting is for *our* benefit, not something we do to please God.

So, after nothing but defeat, the Lord led me to begin a fasting regimen. When I looked this word up in *Webster's Dictionary*, I saw that "regimen" means a system of diet, exercise, etc. for promoting the health. This began a regimen for promoting my spiritual health. Finally, I discovered how to break the power of my flesh through the discipline of regular fasting. I started with the easiest meal for me to fast, which is breakfast. The first of the week seems like a good time to begin anything whether it be a diet, a new exercise routine, or whatever. So this is how the fasting routine went: I fasted breakfast on Monday, lunch on Tuesday, dinner meal on Wednesday, and breakfast on Thursday. By not eating from Wednesday noon to Thursday noon there is a 24-hour fast involved. As I implemented this schedule, there was no problem getting up for my time with the Lord. It worked!

I found that by denying my flesh the right to tell me when to eat, how much it wants, and how I wanted it prepared (ha), the grace of God enables me to say "no" to my flesh which helps me say "yes" to God. When I followed this discipline, there was never a vote at 5 A.M. when the alarm went off as to whether I would get up or not. However, when I rationalized, compromised, and ate meals that were supposed to be fasted, there were times that I even got up out of bed thought it over and decided I would rather sleep! Romans 8 is true, my flesh really doesn't care about the things of God or pleasing God!

This 5 A.M. appointment with God changed my life! I am not the same. In my journals it has been recorded how the Lord has led me to deal with circumstances and relationships in my life. But the greatest benefit is the relationship that developed between the Lord and me. As the pressures of life increased, I found this time early in the morning to be my oasis in the desert, being comforted there by the Lord. As adversity has come and I have received His grace, I have overcome it. Discovering how much the Lord loved me made the biggest difference because then my response to His dealings was different. Being in the Scriptures helped me to change my wrong ways of thinking and helped me to become more secure. Hearing His voice and getting to know Him changed me. Becoming a doer and not just a hearer by applying truths as God revealed them to me has made me into a much more confident person.

Lifestyle fasting continues in my life to this day. Unless I embark on a specialized fast for breakthrough, I still fast four to five meals a week. It works! Fasting enables me to set my mind after the things of the Spirit.

Items We Can Fast or Deny Ourselves

- Fast all beverages except water
- Eating out
- E-mail
- TV
- Meals
- Breads
- Hot drinks
- Meat
- Poultry

- Tea

- Coffee

- Earrings

- Dessert

- Chocolate

- Internet

- Facebook

- 2nd helpings of food

- Dairy products (milk, cheese, yogurt)

- Junk foods (chips, snacks, salty food)

- Magazines

- Cell phone

- Denial of what I would want to eat (i.e. in lieu of what I would choose, I might eat oatmeal every morning for a week)

Formerly, my flesh dictated to me what it wanted to do. I'm sleepy, I'm hungry, I'm mad, I want to get even or I don't feel like going to church. But through the habit of fasting, I now have a very disciplined life. My flesh does what *I* want it to, not what it wants to do.

Fasting for Breakthrough!

Years ago I really reached a point of desperation. It still amazes me that it took so long to get desperate. But, the passivity that had been on my life had robbed me of any urgency to move forward. And I had languished in what I have coined "one day" faith. For instance, *one* day my prayers will be answered, *one* day the prophetic words given me will be fulfilled, *one* day I'm really going to get into the Word. I found out that "one day" faith is not faith at all! I didn't know this was counterfeit faith and had wondered why in the world the Lord was not moving in my life.

So much time had passed. Days turned into months and months into years and still I'd gotten nowhere! I have discovered God is not motivated to act on my behalf based upon my having a "need." True faith in God is what moves Him! Believing what He has said is what He is looking for!

So year after year had passed and my destiny kept calling and I kept telling it "I'm coming!" "Be there in a minute!" "One of these days..." and things like that (not really conscious of what I was doing). Then, I began seriously asking the Lord how to fulfill the things He was calling me to do since I was an utter failure, powerless to change my ways, and yet seriously wanting to go forth in my destiny. One morning, I woke up hearing these words over and over, "Don't be a coward. Be led by the Spirit. Be available."

In obedience to the Lord, I went to the flea market that morning. I started to argue with Him that I had just gone to the flea market the week before, but the words rolled through my mind once again: "Don't be a coward. Be led by the Spirit. Be available." It seemed I was being led by the Spirit! When I got to the flea market, the first table I walked up to had a brand new book entitled *Fasting for Breakthrough!* This book inspired me to begin a 21-day fast for breakthrough, and subsequently the writing of this chapter. Now I am amazed at the faith still being released in my life to believe what God has said!

It was like I had awakened from a stupor. At the end of the fast, I felt new freedom had come in the area of faith! I wrote in my journal, "I now know that I can do all things through Jesus Christ!" I feel that this is one of the most important keys to spiritual freedom that I have discovered. Fasting for breakthrough not only affected me, but those in my family that I had prayed for during the fast. So, I prayed and wrote in my journal, "Lord, cause me to run over the obstacles that have seemed so impossible to surmount!"

As I prepared for this fast, I needed to determine specifically what I wanted the fast to accomplish. My target was to see break-through for my family members. We have all been Christians for years. My husband and I were saved and Spirit-filled early in our marriage. Therefore, our children grew up in the faith and all have had numerous experiences with the Lord. They are all now adults and have been Spirit-filled since they were young children. We all believe in and have been recipients of personal prophecy, which we believe has revealed some of the things the Lord has in store for our futures. Many people have discredited the prophetic ministry because they had come this far (like we had) and nothing had happened. I have come to find that a prophetic word is like buying a coat for a young child in the size that will fit when he or she is a teenager. The coat hangs or is packed away until the child fits the coat. The growth we Christians have, takes place in character development, such as in integrity, being teachable, being repentant and maturing to the point that we are not "hearers" only, but doers of the Word. *We* must be changed to fit the prophecy. That is the price-tag on obtaining what the Lord has spoken to us.

In spite of having been Christians for such a long time, it seemed to me that we were all on our own individual treadmill, constantly walking but getting nowhere! Desperation caused me to do something that I hadn't done before. I began to fast and pray for a breakthrough for all of us. The reason I went on the fast for a breakthrough was for us to get off our treadmills! I specifically wrote down what I wanted the fast to accomplish in each of our lives. I prayed about what I would deny myself that would be a sacrifice, but such that I could continue to live and work as needed. I looked up the fast Daniel did when he needed to hear from the Lord and get wisdom on a vision he had.

I ate no pleasant bread, neither came flesh nor wine in my mouth, neither did I anoint myself at all, till three whole weeks were fulfilled. (Daniel 10:3 ASV)

One thing I had previously learned was that a commitment in the mind can be contested with thoughts and I have been known to lose the battle in the mind! I knew this decision had to be a heart decision not just a head decision. I prayed and asked the Lord to enable me to make a heart decision and He did. It was settled.

The following are two of the results of the fast:

• One daughter, who had a job that seemed to be going nowhere, had a dream that was specific direction to go back to the university and get her Master's degree. She gave notice on her job and followed through and got her Degree!

• One son had a problem with authority and God arranged a series of encounters with people in authority that totally changed his heart!

These are the steps in preparing to fast for breakthrough. The preparation may take a few days.

1. Determine what you want the fast to accomplish and write it out.
2. Decide what to fast.

3. Decide how long it will last.

4. Pray that it will be a heart decision, not just a head decision.

5. Set the start date. I personally like to begin things on Monday.

During the fast – in your prayer time, while driving down the road, while doing your daily activities, and whenever it comes to your mind – pray to the Lord what you want the fast to accomplish. Speak to the things that are hindering and declare that they are finished! Praise the Lord for the breakthrough!

I was so amazed at what began to happen in my family, that upon completing those 21 days, I immediately prayed about what to fast for the next 21 days! This turned out to be a practical and successful means to move forward!

Chapter 16

God Is Working On Us and Uses Circumstances in Our Lives

*W*hat happens when our state of affairs contradicts what God has promised?

Our Story

For my husband, the promise was great financial blessing. As a new Christian, he had powerful prophetic words spoken over him concerning wealth. One prophetic word in 1979 declared, "You will *not* be poor," (I should have recognized the foreshadowing), but "money will come in in big chunks and go out in big chunks." That sounded like good news. However, great prophecies have great price tags. We had to go through preparation to handle the wealth that God had spoken about.

We did not know the Bible very well, and my husband was advised by an elder in our church, whom he respected, that God did not expect us to tithe when money was tight. This was bad advice.

Later we found out that in the book of Malachi, God said to give Him what is His, and He will open up the windows of heaven and pour out a blessing.

Financially, things really got worse for us instead of better. In the beginning, I thought, *Even though circumstances are tough, just any day now a breakthrough will come just like God promised.* It didn't happen that way. Over the years, God dealt with, among other things, personal integrity in business, motives, and generational curses that were hindering the blessing.

I tried just accepting the hard circumstances as God's will. This mindset was passive. It seemed easier to just accept the situation than to question God. We came under a spirit of poverty. Eventually I tried escape through movies and television. That was futile because relief from stress was only temporary. There were years that I did nothing, and then I fasted, prayed, declared, got mad, cried, and prayed some more. The financial struggle period was embarrassing, humiliating, and resulted with loss of reputation. We lost our credit, were looked down on and felt sorry for. My goodness! I love what I learned through all that I went through but wouldn't want to repeat it for anything!

So passivity was a bad idea and also not obeying God's Word was a bad idea. It was challenging and there were battles in the mind. Now I realize that God gave the "Father of Faith," Abraham, as an example for us. He was promised a son and for years his circumstances contradicted what God had promised him. But he believed God... and one day the promise was fulfilled.

We went through ups and downs, and by God's grace made it through it all. Once we got a revelation of what God required from us financially, we tithed and gave offerings as the Lord directed us. Our struggles continued.

We Found Out What It Was Like to Be Harassed by Bill Collectors

To harass is to persistently bother, annoy, or attack somebody. Wow – I've experienced harassment. We had caller-ID on the phone so for many calls, seeing a bill collector's name triggered responses from family members: "I'm not answering it." Then whoever else was in the house said, "Well, I'm not answering it either!" I even put my cellphone on vibrate so that I didn't have to listen to the phone ring and ignore collection calls.

The most illustrious story is an automated call I received years ago. The phone rang. I answered it and was addressed by a recording on the other end. The man stated the company name and then said,

"Your account with us is past due, what do you intend to do about it?" Then the voice was silent.

I mutely held the phone.

Then the automated voice said, "Silence is *not* an answer."

Oh! I hung up the phone, totally intimidated by a recording! I was dumbfounded that a machine was asking me a question and waiting for an answer.

During the final season of our financial breaking, we received collection calls that had been out-sourced to India. They called every single day. On each call we had to verify all our information: "What is your address? Why are you late? When are you going to make a payment?" Then they made mild collection threats. To say to them, "I told you people the same thing yesterday," only seemed to encourage their aggressive phone training.

Finally I had enough and wrote letters to every bill collector that was making harassing phone calls and told them that according to FCC, I could request that they no longer call me and that they had to cease and desist. After they received the letters, the phones were quiet again. Wow. What a relief! Eventually we got caught up and everyone was happy with us.

Breakthrough finally came. But just four months before it happened, I had a dream. At the time we owed $10,000 in back payments on our house and the Loan Modification we had applied for was still not approved. It was a dark dream, which means it didn't originate from the Lord. In the dream, my husband and I had a place to sleep outside next to an office building under a blanket that was woven from leaves. This dream revealed the enemy's plan to cause us to lose our house and be homeless. So we prayed the opposite thing!

What Is It Like to Get a Prophetic Word in the Midst of This?

We had many prophetic words before this personal trial got underway promising prosperity and success no matter what it looked like at the present. As time went by we were worn down under pressure. To get a word from the Lord during such a season is like a cold cup of water to a weary traveler. It is especially meaningful if the person giving you the prophetic word does not know your situation. However if you have "ears to hear" you won't care who delivers the word – whether they know you and your situation or not. You will know it is the Lord speaking a word of encouragement not to give up.

If you are a person who has received previous prophetic words, I highly recommend that you get them out, dust them off and declare them aloud. If they just seem like words on paper, then I suggest that you treat unbelief and doubt as mortal enemies and begin to address them as such, taking authority over them.

Fasting is very helpful to break the power of unbelief. Fast something: coffee, desserts, one meal a day, fast a whole day, whatever the Lord leads you to do. If you have a health condition, fast something that would not be a threat to your health. There are suggestions in the chapter on fasting. Faith will arise if you declare the Word of the Lord aloud. Press on until you are free to believe again! Re-word the prophetic declarations that were made over you and put them in "first person."

My Story

By declaring and agreeing with what the Lord has spoken over me and my family, my faith began to arise and take hold of the promises once again. I declared the truth and it reassured me that my faith was not in vain.

I declared, "My hope is in You. I will not be moved! Through the storm, my hope is in You!" He gives hope to the hopeless!

What Was It Like to Have Something Serious Added on Top of the Financial Difficulty?

It happened to me. Right in the battle for financial survival, another calamity happened in my family. I wanted to "go home."

I thought, *Forget it, God. I'm done. I don't want to live anymore. I'm serious.*

At this latest news, I was stunned. My mind screamed. My emotions screamed. I could not focus. I wept. Then I wept some more. Then I got alone with God and heard His still, small voice speaking hope and comfort to me. I had a choice. Would I just give up on everything that God had promised? Or would I stick my head in the sand and go into denial that this was even happening? I chose to praise the Lord and declare His Word. Yes, everything that could be shaken in my life was being shaken. But that choice is how I survived. All that was happening to me did not add up to *my view* of Christianity. What ever happened to "happily ever after?" I know the Bible never promised that. Note I said *my view*.

At times like this we find out how well we handle stress! We are in the process of being conformed into the image of Jesus. That means that things in us that are not like Him get exposed and that's what happened with me. Part of this process is having everything shaken to see what is really there. What remains is what is of God. All that is not of Him gets shaken off us.

What Helps During Times Like This?

- Hearing a testimony of what God has done for someone else really helps. It gives us hope. We must never devalue the importance of sharing our overcoming stories with others.

- Spending quality time with the Lord was the greatest source of strength and help for me. Hearing and reading His written Word and being able to hear His voice and receive His love and comfort is how I made it through. I would have perished without it.

- Also helpful is going back over previous prophetic words and reminding myself of what the Lord had spoken and then declaring that I am not moved by what my eyes see, helped to renew my mind.

- It is good to worship and to praise through all the things that come our way. It magnifies God in our eyes. It magnifies what we expect and causes our faith to arise. It causes us to recognize that someone greater than us is in charge! When we come into agreement with what our spirit knows about God, we feel it. We sense the reality of the way it really is.

What Makes Matters Worse?

- Listening to negativity from others only feeds doubt that anything will change.

- Self-pity really cripples us in our walk of faith. Feeling sorry for ourselves is an awful condition to be in.

- It will make matters worse if you neglect reading the Bible, fasting, and prayer. This is no time to become passive.

Where Do You Find Peace in the Midst of It?

Only with time in the Lord's presence and reassuring ourselves with His written Word, is *the peace that passes all understanding* released to us. Jesus is the Prince of Peace.

I remember hearing years ago that we don't find out that God is all we need, until we find out He is *all* we've got. What a statement.

Because of my former trials and experience, I have some understanding of finances as God views them. My husband and I have been through every stage in the area of finances. We have been high and low a few times. We've been bankrupt, homeless, and finally restored and blessed abundantly. We learned a lot along the way.

Those who are carnal and only earthly-minded will want to focus and spend money only on their own desires. God cannot trust them with over-abundance for it will probably lead to their corruption. But the one who begins to get revelation of the Kingdom of God – not just as a theory but sees the reality of it – and knows that the purpose of having wealth is for God to use, will have a different life. If this person's heart is anchored in God and they begin to see with heaven's perspective, they can be trusted with earth's resources because it will be used just as the Father wants it. When it comes to material wealth, I have found that it all depends on the heart.

The Tithe

I have heard some say that tithing is merely an Old Testament command. However, in Matthew 23:23 and Luke 11:42, Jesus is talking to the Pharisees. He did not say tithing wasn't required anymore, He was correcting their religious focus – where they cared very much about prideful religious activity.

[…] You give a tenth of your mint and dill and cumin, and have neglected and omitted the weightier (more important) matters of the Law – right and justice and mercy and fidelity. These you ought [particularly] to have done, without neglecting the others. (Matthew 23:23, AMP)

Jesus taught a parable in Luke 18, beginning in verse 9. He mentions tithing in the story. In Hebrews 7:5 (AMP), Paul is teaching and says, *And it is true that those descendants of Levi who are charged with the priestly office are commanded in the Law to take tithes from the people […].* In verse 8, he continues, *Furthermore, here [in the Levitical priesthood] tithes are received by men who are subject to death; while there [in the case of Melchizedek] they are received by one of whom it is testified that he lives [perpetually].* (AMP)

In Malachi – the last word in the Old Testament, God said people were robbing Him when they did not bring all the tithes (the whole tenth of their income) into the storehouse. Then Jesus said, "I did not come to do away with the Law but to fulfill it." In the atonement, He took on all our sins, and in His suffering He paid for our healing, but did not pay our tithes for us!

Beyond the Tithe

In 2 Corinthians 9, this is about offerings. An offering is what we give beyond the tithe. This is where the abundant blessing comes from. This is where the law of sowing and reaping comes into effect in finances.

Paul understood the spiritual law of giving. We often quote (out of context) Philippians 4:19, *My God shall supply all your need according to His riches in glory by Christ Jesus.* Paul was writing a letter to people who had given contributions for his needs (see verses 14 and 16). In verse 17, he was happy for them that they would have a *harvest of blessing*! Then he said the verse we quote so freely. No wonder their needs would be so readily met by the Lord. (I'm quoting the Amplified Bible.)

SECTION THREE:
HOW TO MOVE ON

Chapter 17

Passivity

My Story

$\mathcal{S}$ometimes we have a bad day all day long and never fought back. It may start with a negative comment from someone. If we are passive, that comment can affect us all day long.

When I discovered this, I made a declaration that I will not remain passive when the enemy attacks me. I will stand firm in the Word of God. I will rise up. I won't lay down let him run over me, back up and do it again! Do you know there is a Scripture about that?

In Isaiah, we read that the enemy says, *"Lie down that we may walk over you." You have even made your back like the ground, and like the street for those who walk over it* (Isaiah 51:23 NASB). But then it goes on to say, *Shake yourself from the dust, rise up, o captive Jerusalem; Loose yourself from the chains around your neck, o captive daughter of Zion.* (Isaiah 52:2 NASB)

The dust is from being captive. We're sitting there waiting on God and the dust is settling on us. Instead we should be moving and cooperating with God. The Lord told me that I tolerated things that I dislike and disagree with, to operate in my house and my life without any interference from me. That is passivity. We must compel the enemy to give up and back off or he will bluff us into a "waiting on God" mode.

The definition of the word "passive" means to be inactive, submissive, and unreceptive.

- Inactive – It causes us to be inactive in that we think we are waiting on God to do something when much of the time He is waiting on us. We may have received prophetic words and promises from God's Word. I've heard people say, "God said it and He will do it." Yes, God is faithful to His Word, but, look closely at the prophetic words. If it says "As you spend time with Me in My Word, then this will happen," there is a condition to the promise that must be met. We usually need to make changes in order for prophetic words to be fulfilled. We especially have to grow in the area of our character. Prophetic words are an invitation to what God wants to do in our lives. Promises from the Scriptures that we are holding onto must be contended for and our faith will be tried and we must persevere in prayer.

- Submissive – The song recorded by Doris Day illustrates this very well. "Que sera sera, whatever will be, will be..." In passivity, we submit to all circumstances as if they were God's perfect will. We begin to look at occurrences as normal when it could be the enemy delaying things or hindering. Examples: we go out and find that we have a flat tire. We get sick. Spill something on our clothing. A prayer for someone's salvation has yet to be answered so we think it must not be time for them. What if they are stuck and no one fasted and prayed for their deliverance from the snare the enemy set for them?

- Unreceptive – When we are passive we are unreceptive to the conviction or direction of the Holy Spirit who is our helper, teacher, and friend. Included in being unreceptive is rationalizing and excusing our behavior when the Holy Spirit wants to change something in us. We also talk ourselves out of obedience to the Spirit because we may not like how it may turn out. We must not *reason* our obedience away.

How do you know when you are passive in lieu of being in faith and trust and at peace? Our will is not engaged when we are passive. Nothing is urgent. Faith is not exercised by a passive person. Joy is our faith gauge as to whether we are resting in faith. Passivity is just that – passive – not actively taking part. We tending to submit or obey without arguing or resisting. "One day" faith is not faith at all. Believing that *one day* God's promises will come to pass, and everything will work out, is not active faith.

Some ways we are passive:

- Prayer – One reason we become passive in prayer is that we get weary in the waiting time between standing for a promise to be fulfilled and the manifestation of that promise. The Bible tells us not to be weary in well-doing for in due season we will reap if we don't faint. In weariness it is easy to get into unbelief. The Scriptures say that hope deferred makes the heart sick (Proverbs 13:12 NKJ). We may think, what's the use? My prayers don't seem to be getting higher than the ceiling. God must be mad or has forgotten about me. Example of prayer that is passive: "Lord, I have family members that are unsaved. If it be Your will, I ask You to save them." Or "I've turned them over to You, Lord. I know that You love them even more than I do." The god of this world has blinded their eyes. Who is going to pray for them if you don't? A good way to pray: "Lord, in the book of Acts, You said to the jailer that he could be saved and his entire household and You are no respecter of persons so I stand on that promise and believe You will save my loved ones." "For my family, You are leading the blind by ways they have not known, along unfamiliar paths You are guiding them; You are turning the darkness into light before them and making the rough places smooth. These are the things You are doing; You will not forsake (abandon or give up) them." (Isaiah 42:16)

- Fellowship with the Lord – We have not fought to find our time with Him. We cannot afford to be passive in this area. He is our utmost necessity. This is why our daily time with the Lord in prayer and the Bible is so necessary. It builds the relationship and our confidence. We need to converse with the Lord and write down what He says to us.

- Reading and meditating in the Scripture – Lord, I repent for not reading Your Word. It is spirit and life to me. I repent for prayerlessness and procrastination, apathy in spiritual things and passivity!

- Money problems: a passive prayer: "Lord we don't have enough money at the end of the month. I know You are probably testing us to see if we really love You, and if You wanted us to have more You would give us more." God's Word has principles of sowing and reaping, promises for tithers, and much more is said regarding finances. We must contend for the promises, not passively wait for them to come to us. We are in covenant with God and He honors faith. He promises that whatever we sow we will reap. It takes sowing in faith on our part and standing through testing in order to see the results. A farmer doesn't plant one day and reap the next.

As I became aware of how passivity ruled me, I wrote out a declaration to change my mind and break the enemy's assignment against me. I declare it aloud so I hear it, and the enemy can hear it, too!

Make This Declaration:

- I declare that I will not be passive and let the enemy run over me. I am aggressive and persistent and I take the kingdom by force! I will live my life on purpose! Passivity, go!

- I shook off the dust, removed the chains from my neck and have risen up in faith and newness of life! I no longer serve the god of this world. Old things have passed away and behold! All things have become new (adapted from Isaiah 52:2).

- The enemy is _not_ stronger than the Lord in me. Greater is He that is in me than he that is in the world!

- I break through and break out of whatever is restraining me. I loose myself from the hindrances and will not sit passively while this is going on! I stir up my faith and take hold of the eternal thoughts that are higher than this earthly plane. I break the power of passivity and complacency and command my day! The world is not taking me for a ride. Any old dead fish can float downstream.

- I will follow You. You do **not** tolerate the enemy's oppression! You are **not** weakened by his persistence! You are victorious in every battle. You crush Your foes. For those who fully follow You, You fight for them! Yes, You will fight for me! If You did it for Your people before the cross, You will surely do it for me. Not because I keep the law, but because I put on Christ and His righteousness and obey Your voice. Listen and obey – there is no other way.

God will turn the tables on the enemy if we break our consent to live in passivity.

Prayer: Lord, I submit my life to You and will be honest with myself and You. I pray for all self-justification, reasoning, excuses, procrastination, and self-deception about the condition of my own heart, to be removed in Jesus name. I renounce all cooperation with the enemy by defending myself and saying I'm really not that bad when I compare myself to others. God, I want to respond to You without making excuses. Lord, I repent for small faith, lazy faith, inactive and unexercised faith. I repent for being passive and ask You to set me free, in Jesus name.

Chapter 18

The School of the Spirit and Being Graded by the Lord

We have been in training and preparation for the time we live in right now. All the things that happened, all the people we interacted with, all the good and the bad circumstances we found ourselves in have helped prepare us for such a time as this. If we will let the Lord redeem the mistakes, the time, and the circumstances, we'll see what can happen. Think of what the word "redeem" means – "to make something acceptable or pleasant in spite of its negative qualities or aspects." (Encarta)

To reach our full potential we need to learn what the Holy Spirit attempted to teach us during this process. We have been in the school of the Spirit. The purpose of a natural school is to educate and train a person so that they will have the fundamental knowledge and skills to operate at a certain level in this world. The parallel is that there is a school of the Spirit to prepare us to walk in our destiny and operate with a fundamental knowledge and skill in the Kingdom of God. It is possible that we don't understand what we are being prepared for and we could stumble right into the perfect will of God.

There are things that I've been trained in by the Holy Spirit and the Lord let me know He was evaluating my progress, and what subjects they were. This evaluation and giving of a grade was to see if I needed further training. This is one school we don't flunk out of. If we don't pass, we just keep taking the "course" until we get it right.

These are a few of the subjects He graded me on:

Forgiveness

Love

Obedience

Submission

Intercession

Fear Management

Diligence

Discipline in daily life

I was surprised at how He graded me because even though I don't feel all that successful, He is looking at the heart to see if I learned something.

Here is how it works: someone offends us in what they said or what they did. If we choose to forgive them, we are growing in forgiveness and if we do not withhold love from them, we are growing in love. We are also growing in obedience since we obeyed the Lord's command to forgive. The grades are a read-out of what we did as these things were tested.

What Does It Take to Go to A New Level in God?

We must get desperate enough not to keep going around the same mountain. When we find that we are in exactly the same place as a year ago and nothing has changed, we must do something.

What does it cost?

- Resistance – There will be resistance regarding going to the new level. It is not to the enemy's advantage for you to go to a higher level of faith, fruitfulness, power, and fellowship with God! So it would behoove him to pick out a weakness you have and begin to go after it if for no other reason to distract and discourage you.

- Time – We need to ask ourselves, "What is important that I am spending my time on and what is not important? Meetings, because we are hungry for more, can keep us running all week long. The "more" we are seeking is really met in the one-on-one time with the Lord. I've found that to be the most satisfying, healing, restorative, empowering thing in my life – intimacy with the Lord. We must fight for our time with Him. It is in His presence that we are changed. It is by hearing Him speak to us that we receive faith and life. It is as a result of His affirmation that we know we are loved as we are just because we are His children and it is His nature to love.

- Prioritization – We must reprioritize our lives. What is important?

- Reality check: What is our motivation? Maybe what motivates us in other areas is lacking in this important area. Do we care if we move on? Are we apathetic, complacent or passive? Are we afraid to leave our comfort zone? Do we need emotional healing? It will be exposed as we move to the next level. Things we tolerated in ourselves will come to light and need to be dealt with. What is our source of comfort? Sometimes there are other things that we turn to when we really need to run to the Lord for comfort and healing. Examples are escape through movies, drinking, shopping, etc. Learn how to recognize when you go to other things. Here again we must use the power of choice and ask the Lord for help.

- Discipline – We need this in our lives. Start small. Don't begin with, "From now on, I'm going to fast two days a week (even though I don't fast at all now). And I'm going to spend one hour with the Lord every day (even though I'm not spending any time now)." It is taken in slow steady advancement. Consistent progress is also an encouragement to us. It is better to spend 15 minutes every day for a week consistently than set an unrealistic goal and become disappointed because we don't meet our goal!

My Story

One morning years ago, I was really upset with myself because I hadn't had my time with the Lord. Once again, I had turned off the alarm and gone back to sleep.

The Lord said, "You haven't fallen short of My expectation. You have fallen short of *your* expectation."

I sighed. I thought the Lord was disappointed in me, but I was disappointed in myself. That really helped me. I am my own worst critic in seeing my faults and also my own worst enemy in that I work against myself much of the time. For instance, if I say I want to rise early before everyone else so I can have a quiet time, I cannot be my own enemy and stay up too late the night before! I can't say that my goal is to exercise regularly and not schedule exercise into my life. I can't say I am going to write an article and never take pen in hand or sit down to type! Come on! A good dose of realism is what I needed. Self-condemnation doesn't need a slot on my schedule! It volunteers to fill in anywhere!

We need active faith to believe we can move up to a new level, not just believe that "one day" it will happen. All the things of the spirit are apprehended (caught, understood, and appropriated) by faith. That is not just a theory. We apprehended our salvation by faith. We heard the truth about it and believed it and began a new life as a born-again believer. It is that way about all the things that God says or that He provided for in the atonement. Isaiah 53 tells that He paid for our sin *and* our healing. Healing must be appropriated by faith, also.

- We must war a good warfare with the prophecies and Scriptures. Write them out. Declare them and agree with them. It means we are agreeing with what He has said.

- What conditions are required? For example, if the prophecy says, "As you get into My Word, you will see...," the condition is that you must be in the Word.

- What is in my way? What is hindering me?

- Know that it will take God's help. We cannot make it happen. It is by grace we are being saved. Along with unmerited favor, grace is the ability to do what we cannot do for ourselves.

- We can cooperate and speed things up. "Unbelief" definitely is not cooperating!

• Remember we are not hanging around, killing time, waiting on God. He is waiting on us.

What Does Time Have to Do with It?

Time is something we are aware of each day as we check our watches to see whether it is time to go to work, if our favorite show is on TV, if it is time to leave for an appointment, or cook dinner, or pick up the kids or go to the movie. But the passage of time in large recognizable increments seems to elude us.

We start to become aware of time passing when we are waiting on the Lord to fulfill a promise and another year has passed. We notice the time when we are in a crisis and face a deadline and give Him until Friday to come through for us.

One of the things that causes change in us, is dealing with the time element. It exposes our impatience, our doubts and fears, and our level of faith. Issues come to the surface that need to be dealt with. We need endurance and patience and this how it is developed.

What time is it on God's time clock? In Ecclesiastes it states there is a time for everything under heaven. There are things that we have done that caused delay in answers to prayer, but there is also God's timing. For instance, in the fullness of time a deliverer, Moses, was raised up in Egypt.

Every word of the Lord is tested.

It is tested to see if the enemy can stop it.

It is tested to see if time passing will make it too late.

It is tested to see if negative circumstances can prevent it and in the meantime, *we* are tested.

Joseph had a dream from the Lord. He went through the betrayal of his brothers, was in a pit, sold as a slave and put in prison. He is an example for us: *Until the time that his word came: the word of the Lord tried him. Then the king sent and loosed him;*[...] *he made him lord of his house and ruler of all his substance.* (Psalm 105:19-21 KVJ) God watches over His Word to perform it. We can count on it.

Why Is It So Important That We Hear the Voice of the Lord?

It is imperative that we hear what the Lord is speaking to us. We need instruction, correction, and help in making decisions. But most importantly we need the relationship and the affirmation as a son or daughter of God. It is part of what restores us, heals us, and reveals our life purpose.

God communicates with people while they sleep, with their heads on their pillows and as they are quiet, He speaks. He speaks in parables. He speaks sometimes loudly (through our circumstances). He speaks in mysteries, but He speaks to be heard. He speaks one way and then if we don't get it, He speaks another. He sees to it that His people get the message. He can speak in whispers (thoughts) and He can speak through shouts (circumstances that demand a response). He will communicate.

God speaks in many ways. One way is through impressions, like when we feel impressed to drive home from work and take a different route or we get the urge to call someone and it turns out to be very meaningful. Sometimes we see a bumper sticker or hear a song that speaks to us. What I want to address now is hearing God's voice directly. I don't mean an audible voice. I mean hearing Him speak to our spirit.

A clear conscience enables us to approach God based on His Word. If we confess our sins and repent, our conscious is clear.

Some days we may feel unworthy. On those days, we can say, "I'm coming to You, Lord, based on the blood of Jesus that was shed for me not because I feel righteous or deserve anything." As I mentioned previously it is not based on our feelings.

Who can ascend the hill of the Lord? [...] He who has clean hands and a pure heart [...]. He will receive blessing from the Lord and righteousness from the God of his salvation. (Psalm 24:3-5 NKJ)

Daily we need to press in to hear His voice and write down what He says. The voice He uses is our voice in our mind. He doesn't speak in King James English. He speaks to us in our own way of speaking which sounds just like our own thoughts. We learn to discern whether they are our own thoughts, if God is speaking, or if they are thoughts from the enemy. It just takes practice.

Note:

Any condemning thoughts are not from God.

My Story

Years ago, I reached for a second piece of pecan pie and had a thought that I really didn't need to eat it. I overrode the thought and proceeded to take it out of the refrigerator. Then another thought came: "You say you hear My voice, but are you being selective about what you hear?" I put the pie back. (Perhaps now you know what I mean about the voice in our mind.)

Here is an exercise: Take a sheet of paper and write down a few things you need an answer about. This is a faith exercise. So expect to receive direction. Keep it simple.

Sample:

Who do I need to call or write?

When is my best time to spend in prayer?

What is something I could fast for a week to have a breakthrough? (Hot drinks, Facebook, bread, desserts...)

Now don't concentrate on getting an answer but later glance back at your questions and see if you receive a thought that could be the answer.

Chapter 19

Personal Discipline

What is its value?

Is it frustrating?

What helps and hinders it?

*P*ersonal discipline is absolutely necessary to live a successful life. The discipline of bathing every day, brushing your teeth, and eating three meals seem like simple automatic activities, but they are actually a result of self-discipline. There are people who don't bathe every day, don't brush their teeth regularly, and who either skip meals or eat cake in lieu of breakfast because it was there on the counter. There are those who eat constantly, not restricting themselves to basic meals. So that is how easy or difficult basic self-discipline is.

Without physical exercise our muscles become soft and flabby in lieu of being toned and firm. Without self-discipline we sit for hours and watch television instead of accomplishing the things we dream about doing.

We sit in church and continue to listen to teaching and preaching and don't pursue our own dreams of doing the work of the ministry – which is not necessarily taking a place in a pulpit. Our work of ministry may be working diligently, creatively, to bring in finances for the Kingdom of God. It may be to be empowered to reach people in society that have not been reached. It may be any of a myriad of things.

Are you a student? It takes discipline to study to prepare for tests and to complete projects and assignments. It takes discipline to go to bed in order to get enough rest, and then to get up on time to go to classes. We manage to do what we really want to do. Motivation can be that we will get into trouble if we don't do something or we can be rewarded if we do accomplish something. I think motivation is important.

It is frustrating at times when we lack the self-discipline to do the basic things we know we need to do. This frustration can really turn into a sabotage if we are not careful. "Frustration is a feeling of disappointment, exasperation (anger), or weariness caused by goals being thwarted or desires unsatisfied." (Encarta) Anger against ourselves does not motivate us. We think it will. We talk mean to ourselves (self-talk) like we think it will cause us to "shape up." These ill feelings toward ourselves are very toxic. Periodically I have to take some time to forgive myself. I do it aloud (with no one around) and address the issues that have caused me to be disappointed in myself.

Here is an example: Here is an example: "I forgive myself for not working on the project at hand. I forgive myself for wasting time by doing _____(watching TV, Facebook... – be specific). I forgive myself for talking bad about _____. I forgive myself for disappointing me for not _____." Get specific and clear the slate. Then I pray, "Heal my disappointment in myself, help me in these areas, Lord." Then I feel my joy return. The weight of self-condemnation is off me.

What helps to have discipline? Motivation – we must discover what motivates us. Do we not love ourselves enough to make something of our life? Do we not love ourselves enough to try to look our best? Do we not believe in ourselves and our potential? This could be a problem. We need to have faith to believe what God says about us.

Do you believe the lies the enemy has said about you?

Do you believe the bad and not the good?

Do you feel like a step-child and not a true child of God? Whose report will you believe?

Choose! I will believe the report of the Lord and what He says about me!

If currently you believe the lies, then you must renew your mind by changing it to line up and agree with the Word of the Lord – both the written Word and the *rhema* word. Remember, we are transformed by the renewing of our minds. If you have problem with your faith, then you are dealing with doubt and unbelief, which are spirits assigned to do this particular job. This can be broken through prayer and fasting and treating these spirits as the enemies they are. Address them and take authority over them until the power is broken and then regularly do it so as to enforce your victory.

The Lord has given each of us a measure of faith and if we are not free to believe, then we are being hindered spiritually. This needs to be dealt with. Unbelief greatly hinders us. Jesus said, *Love your neighbor as you love yourself.* If you do not love yourself there is a problem. (Deal with forgiving yourself and begin to declare who you are in God. Declare the promises (turn them into first-person statements from Scriptures. Such as *By His stripes you are healed* being changed into "by His stripes I am healed." *And the God of peace will soon crush satan under your feet* to "And the God of peace will soon crush satan under *my* feet!" Do it aloud and release your words into the atmosphere and most of all into your own ears! Your faith will arise.

What Helps Us to Have Discipline?

- We need to be motivated.

- Loving yourself as God does – which is unconditionally. That means you don't get to hate yourself under any conditions. Forgiveness is key in this area.

- Accountability – It helps to have someone we can answer to.

- Rewards – the sense of accomplishment when a goal is met is great. There are so many areas that we need discipline in and so there are many areas to experience the rewards. Keep your eyes on the goal and any progress made toward the goal.

- And most of all, be your own cheerleader. There was a time when David and his men returned to find that their village had been burned and all their wives and children captured.(1 Samuel 30:1-3) He was devastated by this and his own men spoke of stoning him they were so grieved. He encouraged himself in the Lord. That is the bottom line here. When you are alone in your defeat or *perceived* defeat, there may not be anyone else you can turn to. But just a sentence from the Lord can give you hope and strength for victory. Turn to Him for encouragement, and remind yourself of previous victories.

- Finding out what motivates you is important and then the grace of God is what we must learn to rely on. Some of us have a problem with self-sufficiency. We think we can do it ourselves. This attitude may get us just so far. We all have natural abilities in different things. Some have amazing voices and without effort can sing. Some have a natural ability to organize, lead, serve, are good with technology, good with mechanics, or skillful in the arts. But there is a level beyond our natural ability that we mostly never tap into. That is God's ability to take us and anoint us to do what we cannot do on our own. There are two extremes: those of us who think we can do it and those who think we cannot do it, therefore why try? Grace is needed either way.

My Story

We may even get to the end of ourselves in what we previously could do without extra effort or faith. I first discovered this in cooking. I live in the South. We make biscuits. I discovered one morning that my biscuits didn't even turn out right after years of success. I believe in motherhood. I worked at being the best. No one could criticize me in that area. Then one day I was on a trip and accidently left one of my sons at a gas station and drove on down the highway and didn't discover he was missing for 45 minutes. It was the worst thing that had ever happened to me in my life. I didn't even know the name of the service station where I had gotten gas. I failed at motherhood, even though he was safe and we went back and got him.

I did everything in the world to protect my children from the world's influences and they left home and experimented in the ways of the world and did things they were taught were wrong. I failed at my perceived picture of a good mother. But I forgive myself once again as these things pop up into my memory. I am not perfect. My kids are not perfect. My husband is not perfect. My house is not perfect. Spirit of perfection – get out of my life and go in Jesus name! It's okay if things are not perfect. It has been an imperfect world ever since sin entered in the Garden of Eden. So why would I think my life or family should be perfect?

We can be lazy, depressed, think "What's the use?" Being hurt or disappointed, we may have given up on the dreams. We may also think "Who cares?" All these things can be conquered. I challenge you to rise up and overcome! I encourage you to surmount the obstacles! The Word of God says that there were works foreordained for us to walk in. That means God has dreams for us *just like* we as parents have dreams for our children. Though I have dreams for my children, I don't plan every detail of their lives. I want the best for them. I want them to be healthy, find a worthy mate, have children, to be blessed in their endeavors, and serve the Lord. God's view toward us is similar. That means our hairstyle, how we dress, the car we choose, and what we do with the abilities He endowed us with are up to us. The steps of the righteous are ordered by the Lord. Those in right standing with Him can trust Him to lead them and guide them, but this is an interactive relationship and not to be confused with predestination. He has given us a free will and will not override it. He does know how to hem us in (take Jonah for example). But it was still Jonah's choice to go on to Nineveh.

For I know the thoughts that I think toward you, says the Lord, thoughts of peace and not of evil, to give you a future and a hope. (Jeremiah 29:11 NKJ)

Breaking the Poverty Mentality

We Are Not Waiting on God. He Is Waiting on Us.

My Story

We found ourselves in a real financial predicament. The year 2000 was difficult. Business had dried up and we sold our house in December right before it went into foreclosure. We rented a beach house for a few months. Then my husband made a deal with someone to do seawall work in trade for six months on his 55' boat. As it turned out we spent a whole year on it. On 9/11 when the Towers fell that is where we lived.

Even though we obtained a municipal contract for construction, we had little income and were so far behind in our bills that our vehicles were repossessed. When the contract ended we had no income and we both were unemployed. My husband went to work doing maintenance and I took a part-time bookkeeping job.

The boat had satellite hooked up so we spent many hours watching TV, waiting on God to come to our rescue.

Finally, in desperation I asked God what to do. He said to me, "You are going to have to give your way out of this one." So I continued tithing on my $200 a week part-time job and began giving away 10%.

I decided to create a "giving garden." I drew the outline of a garden on an index card. Each time I gave the extra money away, I wrote on my 3" x 5" card what the seed was planted for. I sowed for new clothes, a vacation, and a *paid for* car that no one could take away from me. The card filled up with circles, each one marked with a specific thing I was sowing for. In God's kingdom, the size of the seed does not matter. In a natural garden, when we plant one kernel of corn it produces a whole stalk with lots more seed to plant! So in faith I did this.

God honored my faith. I found that His principles really work! It wasn't long before my husband got a residential contract for a seawall; we resigned from our jobs and moved into a townhouse. As time went by, one job led to another in the business. The same year I planted my "faith garden," I got hired to do a project that provided the money for us to travel to England to see our daughter who lived there with her husband. I got some new clothes, and before long, I even had a car with no car payments.

In telling this story in abbreviated form, it may appear that it all happened very quickly. It was a process getting our credit re-established, but we were eventually able to buy a new home. We have continued to sow and give beyond the tithe, and our finances have been blessed and increased. God is faithful.

Who would have thought that *giving* was the way to have financial increase? God's ways are higher than our ways!

Chapter 20

A Serious Heart Condition

My Story

When I first came to the Lord years ago, I had such a tender heart toward God and people. I prayed for opportunities to share my faith in Him with others. My desire to see them know Jesus caused me to overcome shyness and fear. But, as time went by and I experienced rejection and misunderstanding, I went from having a heart of compassion to having a hard heart. It was a gradual thing and I was totally unaware of the transformation that was taking place inside me. I no longer felt mercy toward the people I wanted to pray for. This seriously damaged my prayer life. No motivation, no answers to prayer, no seeing my loved ones come to the Lord. A stony heart is not good soil for the seed of the Word to be sown in either. (See parable of the sower/soils in Mark 4:1-20.) Having a hard heart resulted in hindered spiritual growth. It was a terrible place to find myself in!

After quite a few years, the Lord opened my eyes to my condition and I cried out to Him for a heart of flesh in place of my heart of stone. I went outside and selected a stone. Then I did a prophetic gesture by holding the stone in my hand as I repented and laid it before the Lord. I told Him I wanted to trade this stony heart for a heart of flesh.

God says, *And I will put a new spirit within you; and I will take the stony heart out of their flesh, and will give them a heart of flesh; that they may walk in My statutes, and keep Mine ordinances, and do them: and they shall be My people, and I will be their God.* (Ezekiel 11:19-20 KJV)

As the Lord was dealing with me, I found that judging is what caused a hardened heart. When we see a fault in someone or we see someone in sin, what we do with what we see is very important. Sometimes we are hurt by others. The wound we suffer may or may not be intentional, but our response must be the same. We have an opportunity to line up with the "accuser of the brethren" or the "Great Intercessor." Will we agree with satan or Jesus? That is the question. To line up with the accuser, we judge the person, but when we line up with Jesus, we pray for the person without judging them. The verses to qualify this choice are:

- The Great Intercessor: *Therefore He is also able to save to the uttermost those who come to God through Him, since He always lives to make intercession for them.* (Hebrews 7:25 NKJ)

- The accuser: *Then I heard a loud voice saying in heaven, "Now salvation, and strength, and the kingdom of our God, and the power of His Christ have come, for the accuser of our brethren, who accused them before our God day and night, has been cast down.* (Revelation 12:10 NKJ)

If we fall for the trick of the enemy, our hearts become hardened (as stone) because this kind of sin is deceitful. We become deluded into thinking we are okay and don't realize how God feels about what we are doing.

But exhort one another day by day, so long as it is called today; lest any one of you be hardened by the deceitfulness of sin. (Hebrews 3:13 ASV)

There were some things that I had prayed about for years. There were people who had never been changed, and I found out it was because of the judging I was doing in my heart. God promised me that when I repented of this, He would hear me again:

Then you shall call, and the Lord will answer; you shall cry, and He will say, "Here I am." If you take away the yoke from your midst, the pointing of the finger, and speaking wickedness (Isaiah 58:9 NKJ).

The most amazing thing happened. The Lord began to remind me precisely at the moment when I saw something that wasn't right, that I had a choice to make. Would I condemn and judge or pray with compassion? By His grace, I began to make the right choice. In just a few short weeks my prayer life changed and I began getting results. The greatest change came in my heart! I began to have a new confidence that the Lord heard my prayers, which meant I was praying in faith and believing. Things began to happen. I thank the Lord for His faithfulness!

If you want to deal with this issue in your own life, you can get yourself a small stone to use as you pray.

Prayer: Lord, I confess to You that I have judged others instead of praying for them. I ask You to cleanse me of habitually doing this. Give me a heart of flesh for this heart of stone. Soften my heart and give me compassion for others. I want to agree with Jesus and not the enemy. Thank You for hearing and answering my prayer, in Jesus name. Amen.

Chapter 21

Being Connected

My Story

*I*t began with grumbling in my heart about my pastor who wasn't being Spirit-led and who was sorely lacking in humility. It doesn't take long before what is in your heart comes out of your mouth, so little comments began to be expressed by me to close friends. Soon after, in my prayer-time as I expressed my dismay at what was happening with my church, I heard the Lord say to me, "Well, don't go to church then." I was relieved because it seemed I felt worse after a church service than I did before I went. Over the next couple of months I didn't attend church and had peace about everything. My relationship with the Lord was wonderful. I read my Bible daily, prayed, and had joy.

Then in my morning prayer-time, I heard the Lord say, "You are like Miriam." I was happy to be identified with the woman who led the women in a dance with her tambourine on the shores after the Egyptians were drowned! (Exodus 15:20-22) In reality, my tambourine kept rhythm with the music during our church services so I took this as a great compliment. Then He said to me, "You are like Miriam. I put her outside the camp." I was stunned. The story is in Exodus 12:1-14. Miriam and Aaron had begun to speak against Moses. God was angered and in judgment she became leprous. Moses cried out for her to be healed and then she was put outside the camp for seven days. They did not move forward until she returned.

I began to cry and deeply repented to the Lord for my attitude toward the leadership that was in place over me. I even went to my pastor to confess this to him. I reconnected to the church and changed my attitude.

Reconnecting with the Body of Christ

Out of frustration, many people want to withdraw from attending church. We know that the church of Jesus Christ is not a building, but the people, the "called-out body of believers." We have a choice when we are hurt, rejected, abused or ignored by others in the church. Will we stay connected or withdraw?

Some of us have been burned by ministries, leaders, and life in general. There are options open to us. We can keep the bitterness and make vows never to be hurt again or we can get healed and put ourselves back in a vulnerable position once more. Many choose to go into isolation. A few say, "We are going to just have church at home. I feel closer to God now that I've gotten away from organized church." That is quite possible. There were times when I felt awful after I went to church. That still doesn't mean that church is of the devil! It also does not negate the admonition of the Lord not to forsake the assembling together of the saints. We should not quit or leave a church angry or wounded. We need to apply God's principles and receive His healing, and then seek whether we would be better suited to another congregation.

It is disturbing to see some of the things going on in the Body of Christ. Territorialism is rooted in immaturity, fear and insecurity. Control and manipulation have caused many to shrink back from involvement. Some leaders' behavior has intimidated people to the point that they back off and become passive, and think, "What's the use?" The people who make up the church belong to Jesus Christ. *The earth is the Lord's, and the fullness of it, the world and they who dwell in it.* (Psalm 24:1 AMP) Overseers need to remember Jesus purchased the church with His own blood and the people are valuable and precious to Him. Their gifts must not be devalued causing them to think their part is insignificant. Many leaders in their zeal to fulfill *their* vision forget that others have vision, too. This is detrimental to the Kingdom of God.

My Story

As a result of this kind of treatment, I parked my "call" from God in ministry for years and didn't know how to get back and reclaim it. Although I still attended the local church, I was a spectator instead of a participant in the Kingdom of God. I was waiting for someone to give me permission or to reaffirm that I did, indeed, have a ministry. God had to do that, Himself. He restored my dreams and vision and reawakened the zeal to serve my King!

We are instructed to come into alignment with authority. When we do this, it is not the leader we are aligning with as much as it is the position of delegated authority they represent. They are imperfect humans and although they don't see their shortcomings, many times we do. *Obey those who rule over you, and be submissive, for they watch out for your souls, as those who must give account. Let them do so with joy and not with grief, for that would be unprofitable for you.* (Hebrews 13:17 NKJ)

About Being Connected

This subject is not a matter of whether we are going to heaven or hell. It does not have any impact on your destination. This is about the fruit that your life will bear and also whether you are on the path fore-ordained for you.

For we are His workmanship, created in Christ Jesus for good works, which God prepared beforehand that we should walk in them (Ephesians 2:10 NKJ).

This isn't a "fear of God" thing and whether you will miss it and be punished. This is an opportunity to grow, be changed, be challenged, be used, be enriched, and hook up with others that can help you become all you can be!

Regardless of our experiences, the Word of God is still true. Jesus is coming back for a glorious church without spot and wrinkle. The five-fold ministers are to build up the body to the perfecting of the saints to the full measure of Jesus Christ. Hey, we have some growing to do. We have some wrinkles to be ironed out. It takes conflict, sandpaper, iron sharpening iron to be perfected. Not just in our homes but also in church – those imperfect human institutions that were ordained by God. We need a vision of something bigger than ourselves.

So cave-dwelling is really selfish. I've been there. I've spent years there. I've been quite comfortable, even though I was miserable. It was miserable knowing that I was not fulfilling my dreams, my children had been taken captive, our finances were a wreck and we were escaping through television. But I thought I was waiting on God to do something. I didn't even know I was in a cave!

How did I come out? Gradually. I had to be honest with myself that I was afraid to come out. I wanted to go back in the first time things didn't look right or feel right. Although the false peace I was experiencing was comfortable, in this place of retreat I was not alone. Self-pity, passivity, complacency, and lethargy were all sent to keep me company.

So where are you in this? What is the problem? Get over yourself! Get over them!

Prayer: Help me, God!

Note:
That's a great prayer and can be used daily and many times a day whenever it is needed!

I changed because by God's grace I was *willing* to change. I made the appointment with my pastor and by an act of my will, placed myself under spiritual authority. Gradually I began to trust again. Security and courage began to rise in me. Now I am able to tell others how to do this.

What steps need to be taken?

- Forgiveness

- Healing

- Joining ourselves again, by faith.

- Being open and teachable – this is a decision.

- Being open to correction – this is a process that may take some time. Having been hurt by leaders hinders this until we are restored and have a strong desire to be all we can be regardless of what happens.

- We must stop having flashbacks to who did what to us. This is a new day if we are following the Lord!

Part of the reason I was experiencing defeat in the area of ministry was that I was not submitted and accountable to anyone. I joined the church four years previously, was faithful in tithing and attendance, and committed to the intercessory prayer group. I had a wonderful relationship with the Lord and was staying in my comfort zone, like a good little coward. (Smile.)

While attending a class for potential leaders, I heard the pastor say he was looking for people who would be faithful, accountable, committed, teachable and submitted. In that session, I was persuaded by the Holy Spirit that I was guilty of "doing my own thing." I noted in my journal that I needed to make an appointment with the pastor and come under his headship. I realized that I was a spiritual orphan who has had to glean from anyone I could – no mother or father. The Lord is raising up fathers and mothers to mentor now and it is a good thing.

I had come to a place of "just You and me, God." That wasn't God's plan. In His design, we each have a place and a function in the Body of Christ through the local church. Our hurts, fears, disappointments, and isolation serve only to defeat the reason we are placed together. I knew that I had to come out of the cave and submit myself to my pastor and become accountable.

Chapter 22

21-Day Fasting for Breakthrough

Phase 1

Dealing with You

Week 1

*I*t is time to examine your life and get it into focus. Each of us has a destiny – a plan for our life that was designed before the foundation of the world.

> *He has saved us and called us with a holy calling, not*
> *according to our works, but according to **His own purpose***
> *and grace which was given us in Christ Jesus before the*
> *world began...* (2 Timothy 1:9 NASB)

Between where we stand at present and that destiny, are stumbling blocks and what appears to be a mountain of obstacles. We need a breakthrough anointing to be released so that we can move forward. We have dreams and desires in our hearts that God has placed there. But, God would rather have *you* than what you can *do* for Him or accomplish in this life. Phase 1 will deal with restoring your "first love" relationship with the Lord. This plan is to accomplish a breakthrough in your life. In order for it to be effective, there are some key elements that must be present:

- A strong desire on your part to have a breakthrough in your relationship with the Lord.

- Don't be self-condemning but do be honest with yourself as you fill in the blanks.

- Release your faith to believe that God will help you.

God desires a close relationship with you. If you desire a close relationship to Him, this 21-day plan to deny the flesh may be just what you need to tune in to Him. However, there is a tendency for us to get religious and think that we are doing a fast to please God. This fast is not to *get* the Lord to do something and it is not *for* God that we are doing it. This fast is for us as individuals to become more sensitive to the Spirit and to lessen the hold of the flesh. The Bible says the flesh and the spirit are at war with one another.

But I say, walk and live [habitually] in the [Holy] Spirit [responsive to and controlled and guided by the Spirit]; then you will certainly not gratify the cravings and desires of the flesh (of human nature without God). For the desires of the flesh are opposed to the [Holy] Spirit and the [desires of the] Spirit are opposed to the flesh (godless human nature); for these are antagonistic to each other [continually withstanding and in conflict with each other], so that you are not free but are prevented from doing what you desire to do. (Galatians 5:16-17 AMP)

In Phase 1, you will be dealing with removing the hindrances to having the relationship with the Lord that you want. The Bible says, *If we confess our sins* (agree with God), *He is faithful and just to forgive us our sins and to cleanse us of all unrighteousness.* (1 John 1:9 KJV)

What is in your way? What is stopping you from the relationship you want and need with the Lord? Here are some of the things that could be hindering you:

Apathy, laziness, complacency, disappointment in God, unworthiness, guilt, fear of God, feeling unloved, feeling that God is disappointed with you, known sin in your life that you haven't repented of, anger over the circumstances of your life, low self-esteem, fear of rejection, fear of failure, and fear that God will require something of you that you will not want to comply with. These are just some suggestions. Ask the Holy Spirit to reveal to you what is in your way. Use a sheet of paper and list the things that are hindering you.

List what you want this fast to accomplish (example: to be able to read the Bible and understand it, self-discipline, freedom from intimidation, believing that the Lord really loves me, or the ability to break free from a particular sin).

Step 1: (Days 1-3) is a "denial." This is left up to you to find out in prayer what would be a sacrifice for your flesh to give up. (Example: for one person coffee would be a sacrifice, to another television or sweets.) This denial will last for 7 days altogether. After 3 days additional things will be added to the denial. If you do not have an established time to pray already, begin with 15 minutes a day. During that time, get a pen and paper and ask the Lord to bring to your mind things you need to deal with. If things that are painful come up, forgive those that have caused hurt or disappointment and ask the Lord to heal you. Begin to read the four Gospels, put on praise music if you feel oppressed, and talk to the Lord every chance you get. For instance, in your car, when you find yourself waiting in line somewhere, etc. Begin to declare "The Lord is at work in my life." Declare the things you listed as changing.

Step 2: (Days 4-6) Realize that you have honored the Lord with the denial and say "Lord, You said if I would draw near to You, You would draw near to me. (James 4:8) Thank You for continuing to help me with this fast." This next step is *continuing* with what you gave up for the denial and in addition, you fast all starches and desserts (potatoes, rice, bread and desserts). This you do for 3 days. Don't be legalistic – a breath mint is okay, if needed.

Step 3: (Day 7) On this day, you eat only fruits and vegetables. Take some time with the Lord. Pray and ask Him to show you the sin in your life. Repent of all known sin. It is possible that you will see how selfish you have been, or that you need to apologize to someone.

Phase 2
An Anointing to Finish
Week 2

So many times we begin something we feel is very important to our destiny. For example we set goals to be more disciplined, to have order in our life, to set priorities and follow through – only to find we are back where we started and got nowhere! We need an anointing to finish.

If you feel you only scratched the surface in dealing with your hindrances to making progress in your walk with the Lord, please go back and repeat the steps in Phase 1. If you have experienced a liberty in your relationship with the Lord, then proceed to the following steps:

What is hindering you from doing the things you feel are very important, but are powerless to do?

Step 1: (Days 1-3) Again, you will pray and find out what you need to deny yourself for the 7 next days. You are back to normal eating during the first 3 days other than what you are denying yourself.

Take time with the Lord. Ask Him to show you the things that you need to do (some realistic goals). This is different for everyone. Is there a book that you know the Lord wants you to read? Is there a closet you want to organize? Do you need to establish a regular prayer and Bible study time? I threw in the closet because sometimes it is a very practical thing that needs to be done. Procrastination needs to be repented of and its power broken! When you see what you need to do, break down the task and set realistic daily goals and do it. "I can do all things through Christ who strengthens me." Take time to tell the Lord what you are grateful for in your life. Humble yourself. The Lord is near to those who have a humble and contrite heart. And He gives grace to the humble.

Step 2: (Days 4-6) Again you will fast starches and sweets for 3 days along with continuing to deny yourself what you selected in Step 1. Worship the Lord, read your Bible, pray, write down impressions that you get from the Lord. The anointing to finish is being released into your life. Bondages are being broken. *So if the Son sets you free, you will be free indeed.* (John 8:36 NIV)

Step 3: (Day 7) This is a total fast from solid food (liquids only). If you are unable for health reasons, fruits and vegetables are okay. The Lord will reveal the next steps you are to take in making progress. Write down in faith the things the Lord is speaking to you.

Phase 3
Praying for Others
Week 3

Step 1: (Days 1-3) Back to normal eating except for selecting something to deny yourself for the week. Ask the Lord to give you His compassion for others. Ask Him to remove all judging and criticism. Pray in faith for those the Lord puts on your heart. You may begin to understand more about why people act the way they do. You will probably be more sensitive to the Lord and His promptings.

Step 2: (Days 4-6) These 3 days eat only fruits, vegetables, and bread (no meats or desserts).

Step 3: (Day 7) Fast from solid food from sunup to sundown. If you are unable for health reasons, fruits and vegetables are okay.

This completes the 21-Day Fasting for Breakthrough.

Chapter 23

Procrastination

Don't Allow It In Your Life. It Is Time to Move On!

The word "procrastinate" means to let something slide, or postpone it. It indicates inaction. Some people, like me, are driven by perfection. If there was not enough time to do a perfect job, I procrastinated. I also found out in prayer one day that because of delaying my obedience to the Lord many times, this became a trap I couldn't get out of. I dealt with it in prayer and was set free!

Lazy hands make for poverty, but diligent hands bring wealth. (Proverbs 10:4 NIV)

A sluggard's appetite is never filled, but the desires of the diligent are fully satisfied. (Proverbs 13:4 NIV)

Prayer: Lord, I repent for delaying obedience to You, which in reality is disobedience. I repent for putting things off. I want to be diligent. Heal my disappointment in myself over all the wasted time and opportunities. I repent for putting things off. I repent for procrastinating and coming up with excuses for my behavior. I repent for wasting so much time on worthless things. I repent for reasoning my obedience away and now I break the power the enemy has to delay things in my life, in Jesus name. Amen.

Take some time to pray and then jot down some things you know that you need to do that you have been putting off. Keep it simple and realistic! Read the Scriptures below. Confess the Word out loud that speaks to you the most from these verses. Pray to receive the grace to follow through. This is a battle against the flesh, which is hostile toward God. (Romans 8:7) It will take daily standing on and declaring the Word (using your sword), daily praising the Lord in faith for His strength showing up in your life, and then following through with the action that you have set out to do. Expect results!

These Scriptures are put in the "first person" to make a declaration for ourselves.

I labor, struggling with all His energy, which so powerfully works in me. (Colossians 1:29 NIV)

This is my work, and I can do it only because Christ's mighty energy is at work within me. (Ephesians 3:20 LB)

You are able to do exceeding abundantly above all that I ask or think, according to the power that works in me! (Ephesians 3:20 KJV)

I can do everything through Him who gives me strength. (Philippians 4:13 NIV)

The following are antonyms for procrastination and they show what the opposite thing would be. Look at these words! Accelerate – advance – cover ground – move quickly – speed up – move on!

Let's do it!

Forgiving God

My Story

I received devastating news concerning one of my children. I was stunned. I was not expecting it. My hopes for their future were crushed. I wanted to go into denial and say, "This can't be happening!" I knew that would not help. So I turned *to* God, not *away* from Him. The following is not an eloquent prayer. It is a record of me pouring out my heart to Him.

I said, "Lord before I let this cause me to back away from You, I want to be sure I clear the air between us. I know You are God Almighty, maker of heaven and earth. All-knowing and all-seeing and all-powerful are You. I know You could have prevented this 'disaster after disaster' that has taken place with my family. You could have warned me or told me, but You did not. So with all this in mind, I choose by an act of my will to forgive You for not intervening like I would have wanted You to. I forgive You for not warning me or telling me. I receive Your healing of my disappointment and my heart that is broken over this. I need You above all else. I could be dead already and should have been years ago, and I would not have seen this day, but You have kept me here for a reason. So I will keep breathing and keep walking and keep praying and keep warring until Your divine purposes come to pass. I lay down my life. I lay down my dreams of having a normal family. My fantasies of what a normal family looks like have been shaken loose. Thank You for Your love and healing and grace and comfort."

Although this was a very difficult time in my life, nothing came between me and the Lord because of the way I dealt with it. I had the grace to walk through it. I had the presence of the Lord and joy in my heart even though it was necessary to battle in my thought life and pray like never before. A real key is forgiving God for what He has allowed. Some may experience a conflict about the words "forgive God." My own argument at one time was that He is God, He is good, He is sovereign and you cannot have things against Him. Well in theory that is true. But in reality, I know things that happened. He has let people die that I prayed for. He has permitted very difficult trials in my life. So in order to heal what has come between us and for my own good, I will forgive Him. It is human nature to shrink back from those who have hurt us. How close to God do we want to be?

Counting the Cost

Count the cost – salvation is free, but the rest will cost you something. Cost means that it has a price tag. The only "negative" aspect is that sometimes it is a sacrifice which means you will have to give up, forgo, let go, or surrender something. I want to tell you that it is *so* worth it!

Freedom – If we want liberty, a lack of restrictions, and the ability to exercise our free will, there are some steps that must be taken. And they need to be taken at different stages in our growth on the journey with the Lord. At all levels of maturity, we find we still need other members of the Body of Christ.

Keys: Get Help – ask for, seek, or request help. However it is important *who* you ask for the help.

You may need some deliverance – to get released or liberated from demonic influence in your life. Some things are caused by generational things passed down. (Rejection, low self-esteem, unworthiness.) There are many things that will keep us from pursuing God. Fear is one of them. I was afraid of God *and* the devil before I became a believer. The devil was evil and scary, but I had sinned against a holy God and I feared His punishment. I believed that Jesus died for my sins, but in my ignorance did not know that God the Father loved me, wanted to spend time with me, or wanted to show me His love.

Seek counsel (advice, guidance, direction, warning, recommendation, encouragement, and support). Sometimes we need a person (someone trustworthy that would have our best interest in mind) to give us godly advice.

Blessed is the man who walks not in the counsel of the ungodly (Psalm 1:1 NKJ).

- Anointing – spending time with the Lord causes us to be changed into His likeness.

- Intimacy with others – sharing heart to heart. Not everyone can be trusted but that is no reason to think that there is *no one* who can be trusted.

- Intimacy with God – learning to hear His voice. He has kind, wonderful things to say to us. We can share heart to heart with God. He wants us to tell Him how we really feel. In the beginning I thought God was as disappointed in me as I was. I was writing down what I felt like I needed to change about myself. I said, "God, we need to talk about order and discipline." And I heard, "And approval and love." I started to rebuke the devil and then realized it was God in His kindness talking to me, loving me, accepting me in spite of myself.

- Revelation – there is a storehouse of revelation – things God wants to disclose to us. There are amazing things, truths that God wants to reveal, unveil, and make known to us. These things will show us how He views us, things that have happened (the way they really happened), truths in His Word of what has been provided, what He will do, how we are to operate *in* this world and not be *of* it. Just to name a few things that we need revelation for.

- If we want more it will take revelation of many things to secure it for us. If we don't have revelation we don't have a sure foundation. I can say that Jesus loves us, and we may even give mental assent to that assertion. But when we miss the mark in our behavior, do we still believe it? When we are alone, do we believe it? When we have to wait for an answer to prayer, do we still believe it? When He reveals by the Spirit (revelation), nothing can take it away. Nothing can convince us that He doesn't love us. We might not understand what is going on. We might feel unworthy at the moment, but we *know*. That is what it means to have revelation of His love. I have met very few people who were not assured of their salvation if they were truly born-again. They had the revelation that Jesus died for their sins and they heard the Truth that if you say with your mouth and believe in your heart that God raised Jesus from the dead, you will be saved. They had the revelation. And there might be days that you don't act saved or feel saved but there is revelation knowledge that you know that you are saved. Well there is so much more. There is revelation of Christ *in you* the hope of glory! That brings great assurance in serving Him! And in stepping out and believing He is with you because you know He is not only with you, but He is *in you*. Revelation of healing being for you and also for you to lay hands and bring healing to others. Not just something that you do by "faith" but people really get healed!

It Costs More

Now where does the cost come in? Having to ask for help. Getting delivered from the things that hold you back cause you to need someone else's help. It takes humility or desperation to ask for help.

Chapter 24

The Anointing That Breaks the Yoke

The enemy loses his hold over people when they find out the truth of a matter, apply that truth to their lives, and move forward. It all goes back to "You shall know the truth and the truth will set you free." What we don't know really does hurt us.

What is a yoke? It is a wooden cross piece that is fastened over the necks of two animals and attached to a plow or cart that they pull together. (Webster) When we are in bondage to sin we are yoked to something that is compelling us to keep walking with it. We struggle but can't seem to get free.

Another type of yoke is a frame fitting over the neck and shoulders of a person, used for carrying pails or baskets. When we are in bondage to guilt, self-condemnation, shame, false responsibilities, and other things, we become loaded down with heavy burdens.

So how do we get free? In Isaiah 10, God told the remnant of Israel that He was going to set them free from the Assyrians who greatly oppressed them with a heavy yoke of bondage. I have included different Bible translations and will elaborate on them taken from Isaiah 10:27. These different translations inspired me to see the different ways that the yoke gets removed from us.

Outgrowing the Yoke

And it shall come to pass in that day, that his burden shall depart from off thy shoulder, and his yoke from off thy neck, and the yoke shall be destroyed by reason of fatness. (Isaiah 10:27 ASV)

In that day their burden will be lifted from your shoulders, their yoke from your neck; the yoke will be broken because you have grown so fat. (NIV)

This can be interpreted to mean that we can outgrow a yoke and break free by reason of our growth in the spirit! How can I outgrow it? How does a child outgrow a highchair? He eats, he rests, he gets exercise, and he is also destined to grow.

To break a yoke in this manner represents the result of growth as a Believer. You break a yoke of unbelief by exercising your faith muscles and renewing your mind with what God says in His Word. Then the enemy loses his power over you in this area.

Can you identify the yokes in your own life? Fear, insecurity, low self-esteem, pride, jealousy, gossip, fantasizing, anger, lust – you can be free.

Because of the Anointing

*And it shall come to pass in that day, that his burden shall be taken away from off thy shoulder, and the yoke shall be destroyed **because of the anointing**.* (KJV)

There are times that a yoke is broken off of us because of the anointing of another person. Their teaching and impartation into our lives cause us to be set free and to overcome an area where we have been in bondage.

Note:

The word "bondage" carries the connotation of slavery.

Because of the Anointing Oil

*It shall come to pass in that day that his burden will be taken away from your shoulder, and his yoke from your neck, and the yoke will be destroyed **because of the anointing oil**.* (NKJ)

When in Israel, I saw an ancient olive press and it was massive in size. To use it, the olives were first crushed and then put into the olive press. Next they were mashed and pressed and the oil was released, captured, and put in containers. The guide told us that the purest olive oil (and this is the kind that was used in the Temple in Jerusalem when it existed) came from a special one where the whole olives were placed in flat baskets and stacked one on top of another and another and another until the weight alone began to press out the oil. The Lord showed me that the anointing that breaks the yoke for others comes from being in God's olive press. While I was preparing to teach this message a few years ago, I heard the Lord say, "It is finished." I was pondering it and the Lord said, "I am not quoting what I said on the cross. I'm saying that what it took to get you here to where you are right now, is finished. The anointing to break yokes for others by sharing from your heart and teaching My ways has been accomplished."

Some of our freedom comes from receiving the truth and applying it to our lives. Some comes from the ministry of others. But a rich anointing is coming forth in our lives as we are in God's olive press. The pressure, the resistance, the "press," aaah the pure oil that is coming forth from us, even as from a real olive press.

My prayer for you: I pray that you learn to discern the difference between the dealing of the Lord and the oppression of the enemy. I pray that you will come to know how deep and wide God's love is for you! And I pray that every yoke of bondage will be broken in your life and that you will know that God's olive press is really worth it. It is wonderful to have a life that bears fruit in God's kingdom.

Epilogue

Instead of being passive, we are active, aggressive and alive!

We are not apathetic. We burn with the zeal of the Lord!

Instead of complacency, we are dissatisfied with the status quo.

In place of doubt, we live with assurance and certainty.

No more fear. Our God has given us security,

confidence and bravery.

We won't walk in unbelief. We live with faith,

conviction and assurance.

We will no longer be lazy. We are industrious and active.

We will not yield to the enemy's plans.

We will resist him and his ways.

It is time to recover what was lost!

It is time to reclaim all that was taken.

It is time!

It is time to advance!

It is time to step up!

It is time to push through opposition.

It is time to overcome!

It is time to shove our way through the crowd that is either
standing still or coming in the opposite direction.
This is the day and this is hour to press beyond the remnants
of unbelief and wavering faith.
We will not think and reason too much.
We will not look at other people's faces for
approval or disapproval.
We will not walk in pride, thinking we can do it just because
we know what to do.
We will always have to depend on God.
AMEN!